INVISIBLE KILLER
The Monster Behind the Mask

INVISIBLE KILLER
The Monster Behind the Mask

DIANA MONTANE AND SEAN ROBBINS

Library of Congress Cataloging-in-Publication Data
Available upon request
ISBN 978-098886051-3

For information, or to order additional copies, please contact:
TitleTown Publishing, LLC
P.O. Box 12093 Green Bay, WI 54307-12093
920.737.8051 | titletownpublishing.com

Distributed by Midpoint Trade Books
www.midpointtrade.com

Interior design by Jane Perini
Cover design by Chris Hineline of TriggerGraphix
Photo sequencing preparation: Chris Hineline of TriggerGraphix
Printed in the United States of America

Between the desire

And the spasm

Between the potency

And the existence

Between the essence

And the descent

Falls the Shadow

T.S. ELIOT, "THE HOLLOW MEN"

This book is dedicated to:

Bill, Mary Lou and Sean Jones....

and to Marilyn Angel.

> ACKNOWLEDGMENTS <

We have to first acknowledge those friends who brought us, like offerings, parts of the puzzle that was this invisible killer, Charlie Brandt.

Michelle Jones' loyal bff's: Lisa Emmons, Debbie Knight, and Peggy Moore, as well as Suzy Hamilton and Christine Dumouchel. Especially to Diana Raquel Sainz for her incessant and valuable promotion out of loyalty to Michelle and "Miss Gizzie." To Tracy Helfrich's steadfast girlfriends: Nancy Carney, Melanie Fecher, and Colleen Maloney Michie. Charlie's fishing buddies, who were as shocked and appalled by his crimes as everyone else: above all, Jim Graves, who generously brought this story to our attention; and Donald Withers, Mike Savedow and Kevin Shore; also, former roommate Lonie Weiner, who should have been a lady detective. Nick Gelyon and Christopher Duett for their insight and efforts. Niki Mousikos for her patience and Robbins Radiator and Service Center as well as The Shark lounge and Tir na Nog Irish Pub in Daytona Beach Florida. Frank Gunshanan and Maggie Karda for their endless time,encouragement and belief in this process. It didn't go unnoticed.

Then there is "the League of Extraordinary Gentlemen," headed by FBI profiler Mark Safarik; Rick Roth, former Monroe County Sheriff; Agent Dennis Haley; whose wit only matches his experience; Fish Michie, who is as observant as those in law-enforcement; Linda Mixon, Detective Sargeant of Major Crimes; in fact, the entire Monroe County Sheriff's department for their sensitivity about victims. Our good friend, ret. Daytona Beach Chief of Police Paul Crow, thanks for the other suspect. Good friend Kathy Kelly, thanks for the old articles from the *Daytona Beach News-Journal,* which were very helpful. And Lyda Longa, also from the *News-Journal,* for introducing us to one another. To ret. Miami Homicide Detective, Private Investigator Pat Diaz, thanks for your contribution; and to Dr. Michael Brannon, for your insights into the psyche of the monster; to Gina Buell, thanks for your account of "a serial killer on the loose."

To Marta Sosa and Scott Wevley, our deep felt gratitude for all the constant work, and your deep understanding; and a special thanks to Chris Hineline and Triggergraphix for his extraordinary graphic design.

To Mary Lou Jones, a big thank you for your prodigious memory, your gracious and constant availability on behalf of your daughter Michelle, and your large contribution to this story.

Linda Langton, of Langton International, thanks for your grace and patience. And our publisher, Tracy Ertl, of Titletown, for your unwavering faith in this project.

We need to single out, for a special commendation, Special Agent and profiler Leslie D'Ambrosia, who was with us every step of the way, and is one of Florida's state treasures. And to you, the reader, for taking the time to step into our world and explore.

> CONTENTS <

Would You Be Able to
Recognize a Serial Killer?

by Mark Safarik

Could your neighbor or relative be a serial killer? The problem is, even if he was, you likely would not know. There is often a disconnect between the public's perception of a serial killer as an easily recognizable monster and the grim reality of an average-looking individual who commits unspeakable acts of brutality against another human being. Serial killers look and act like our co-workers, neighbors, and sometimes our friends—a fact that is not only uncomfortable, but incomprehensible for most of us. We want them to be recognizably different in external appearance, manner, and affect. Unfortunately, the sad fact is that what makes serial killers so successful at their craft is, in fact, their ordinariness, their uncanny ability to appear normal, to blend in, to be as unassuming as you and I, to avoid drawing attention to themselves, and ultimately to make you believe that they are like everyone else you know.

Jim Graves, a friend and confidant of Charlie Brandt, and former brother-in-law by marriage to Brandt's sister Angela, trusted his instincts about his ability to read people. He thought he knew Brandt. In reflection, what does it say about a person when he has so terribly misjudged the character of someone he called a friend? Jim thought he should have seen, sensed, and realized something that would have opened his eyes. He chose to explain away the sometimes odd behavior of his friend, instead of letting it stand on its own. In the end, he wished he had recognized the clues for what they were.

I saw this scenario many times during my 23 years as an FBI Special Agent, particularly while working as a senior profiler in the FBI's elite Behavioral Analysis Unit, known to most as the Profiling Unit. After spending another dozen years studying, researching, writing about, and interviewing rapists and murderers of all types, I am intimately familiar with the ability of serial killers to deceive almost anyone.

Brandt was a master manipulator, always in control. The psychopathology of his twisted desires lay beneath his superficial personality, well disguised from everyone. Each of us has a public life, the face we show to the world. We also have a private life, which is revealed only to those very close to us. But then there is our secret life, known only to us. To truly plumb the depths of that secret life in a serial killer, you must have the key that unlocks access to that crucial piece of the puzzle. It is extraordinarily difficult to peel back that façade, layer by layer, slowly revealing the depravity that shocks a normal person's conscience.

Jim Graves confided in his friend, Sean Robbins, the story of his friend and brother-in-law, the serial killer. Robbins sought out Diana Montane and together they collaborated on this book.

Diana Montane is an expert not only at finding the key, but at putting the puzzle together. Uncovering the ugly, naked truth about Brandt was a complex task that involved interviewing those who knew Brandt and the victims and investigators who worked the murder cases. Diana in turn reached out to one of my colleagues, Florida Department of Law Enforcement profiler Leslie D'Ambrosia, to help provide meaning, context, and behavioral linkage to some of those missing pieces. Extracting Brandt's puzzle pieces from the investigative reports, crime scene photographs, mountains of collected evidence, and each victim's personal story involved an extraordinary effort. Diana and Sean were tireless in their pursuit to understand a man that almost no one did.

When I lecture and provide expert testimony, I am always careful to explain that the crime can only make sense when considered in its totality, thus providing context to the behavior. Diana and Sean's task was made all the more daunting because Brandt was dead before anyone even knew he was a killer. They have masterfully succeeded in putting Brandt, his life, and his crimes into context, so we get a clear picture of that secret life.

Lastly, every victim deserves her own justice; she deserves to be understood as a person with goals and dreams, with family and friends who loved them. Diana and Sean, in their journey to make sense of the incomprehensible, never forget about the victims. They give them a voice and help us to understand them as people, not simply as a nameless number in the trail of death left by Brandt.

> PROLOGUE <

By Sean Robbins

"**D**id I ever tell you I was related to a serial killer?" This was the question that initiated the idea for this book.

It was October of 2011 and fall was slightly in the air, but not yet falling. Little did I or anyone else know that fall had not only not fully arrived, but had decided to take its seasonal beauty somewhere far away from this peninsula of the strange.

It was around eleven o'clock in the evening when I left the filthy, un-air-conditioned, rat-infested garage where I was living. As I walked to my destination the heat and humidity spoke to me through sweat signals: unless I continued to push forward creatively, this discomfort would forever be the trap I would have to call home. I made my way through the streets that provided the base for many homes with boarded-up window décor. As I came to the end I began to see the glow of the green neon that provided me a cold nightly relief from the unrelenting heat while also allotting me a place to escape into my creative world—and a fine adult beverage.

The sign read "Tir Na Nog," and as I entered I was greeted with the usual bar camaraderie. I grabbed a beer and my regular spot in the corner booth. I took a pull off the pint of whiskey in my pocket, sat back, and let the kaleidoscope in my mind set into a collection of linear thoughts.

That night was like many previous nights; I would sit in the corner booth, let my mind marinate in the alcohol, and then, when I felt ready, I would dive in and begin to continue work on my first novel. I was about an hour in and things were moving along smoothly when my friend, Jim Graves—back then only an acquaintance, approached me.

Jim was a down-on-his-luck yet very talented guitar player who would regularly host a jazz night at the bar. Middle age and the hazards of the trade had sent his body into a painful spin over the years, but even as his physical nature decayed, his mind stayed sharp and optimistic. He had been fighting the good fight for the disability benefits that he had voluntarily paid into, and knew that if he could just grind out the next six or so months, he would get his money and the medical help he needed. Friendly as usual, he came up and said, "Whatcha workin' on, man?" I replied, "Ehh... just this book I've been trying to write." He said, "Oh, cool man. I didn't know you were a writer. Well, if you are ever interested I have a story for you." I said, "Yeah man, I'm always interested," and looked up at him. The last thing I expected to hear him say came out of his mouth next. "Did I ever tell you I was related to a serial killer?"

I wasn't quite sure what to make of this. Jim had absolutely no idea that I have been a very big follower of the true-crime genre all of my life. Also, with such a bold confession I had no idea if anything he was telling me had any validity whatsoever. He went on to explain to me that there was a television special done on his friend, a *48 Hours* entitled "Deadly Obsession," and informed me how I could find it online. I did this immediately, saw that everything he was saying was true, and told him that I would like to try to take on the task of writing a book on the subject. We talked further and I immediately put my other novel to the side and began the research process that would catapult this project into the realm of possibility.

At the same time I had been reading *I Would Find a Girl Walking*, which chronicled the crimes of serial killer Gerald Stano. My introduction to this book was as random—yet as important—as all the other pieces of the puzzle that would become *Invisible Killer: The Monster Behind the Mask*. One of my longtime best friends whom I've known since the age of six, Bryan Beaulieu, had randomly sent me a text message one night a month or so before my encounter with Jim. He explained to me that a girl at his place of work was reading a book about Gerald Stano and that knowing my interest in true crime, he figured he would tell me the title so I could check it out. Gerald Stano had carried out most of his murderous assaults on innocent women here in Florida, the Daytona Beach area being his primary target for the hunting of his prey. While on death row awaiting execution, Stano had reached out to Kathy Kelly, then the police beat reporter for the *Daytona Beach News-Journal*, and in her, Stano found a pen pal of sorts. The letters were the core of inspiration for Kathy and her co-author Diana Montane's book. As I was reading I noticed, within the "images" section of the book, a current photo of Kathy. I decided, if she was willing to talk, she could provide great insight on how to go about writing a true-crime book.

I called local friend and *News-Journal* crime writer Lyda Longa, and asked her if Kathy still wrote for the paper and, if so, if she could get me in touch with her. Kathy informed Lyda that my best option would be to call her co-author to ask for advice. As I looked into Diana Montane's credentials, her resume spoke for itself. She was a well-established crime author, so I fully understood why Kathy had decided that Diana would be my best option. As soon as I got off the phone with Lyda, I dialed Diana's number, and left a message about how I was trying to write my first true-crime book, coupled with the details of how I got her number to begin with. As the following week went on, I continued documenting Jim's story while doing my own research as well. Seven days went by and I decided to call Lyda, who knew Diana better than I, to ask her whether I should try Diana one more time or just let it go. Lyda said that if I didn't hear from her after another day, I should just go ahead and let it go, since Diana was very busy.

I went home and that night, while I was watching Monday night football, my phone began to ring its very obnoxious ring. The caller ID read "Diana Montane." As we spoke I tried to explain to her what I was doing, and why I had called her. Further into the conversation she revealed to me that she had told Lyda that she had got my message, but because of her hectic schedule didn't want to call me back. She then told me that the only reason she did call was because she'd just seen the missed call on her phone, and redialed it to find out who it was.

If my initial research was the catapult that propelled this project into the realm of possibility, then her following words were the cannon that would fire that possibility into the spectrum of synchronized chaos. She went on to explain how she believed that things happened for a reason and that the fact I was the person she'd randomly called back was no accident.

As we continued to talk, we came upon a proposal of collaboration, which I accepted. From then on began a partnership of two very obsessive, ambitious, rapid-fire minds, with a unique combination of styles, that refuse to bend for a story they believe in. Rejections came by the bundle but failure was never an option, and finally we came upon a visionary publisher and the book that now lies in your hands.. Thanks for taking the time to read.

> PROLOGUE <

By Diana Montane

My writing partner, Sean Robbins, began his prologue for our book, *Invisible Killer: The Monster Behind the Mask*, by stating the strange opener his friend Jim Graves had said to him at his favorite bar: "Did I ever tell you I was related to a serial killer?" Jim had been talking about serial killer Charlie Brandt, who had been his brother-in-law and good friend. Jim hadn't suspected a thing.

I didn't suspect this when Sean came to me with the story. Never would I have imagined I would meet such diverse, wonderful people during the course of writing this book.

I will begin with Sean Robbins, who remains a good friend.

When he first showed up at my house with the beginnings of his story, I saw a young, eager, tattooed-from-head-to-toe individual, a typical Daytona boy or biker. He was not that at all, and this became clear from the start.

What he is, is immensely curious, driven, and dedicated to his craft of writing, albeit intensely suspicious of all forms of authority. I could relate. I used to be like that. And I am grateful he still is. I used to be a "hippie"—yes, in quotation marks. Not a commune-type hippie, but a hippie in the Theatre Department at the University of Miami. We used to throw balloons full of paint at walls and call it "happenings," recite poetry, and participate in marches. We also did damn good theatre, and the experience opened my eyes and mind to all sorts of people. I expect eccentricity in artists; in fact, I welcome it. So Sean and I became like cosmic siblings, in a way.

What I wasn't expecting was the rest of the people who came into my life, and have stayed.

I emailed the Michelle Lynn Jones website and received an answer from Peggy Moore, a loyal friend of Michelle's, who said she wanted to help. Of course, at first, folks say they want to help until they realize one's true intentions. And then they really help. I suppose all of these people realized what this was about, and why I was drawn to this story. I wanted to make the victims as fully rounded people, who had lives they should have continued. That nobody had any right to take.

I was also drawn to the story for the same reasons I went into theatre: to explore the human psyche. In this case, I would be exploring the darkest recesses of a serial killer's mind.

Bill Jones, Michelle's dad, was the second one to call. "I understand you're writing a book about Michelle," he said in his gravely soft Southern voice, and then allowed me to speak with his wife, Mary Lou.

I wasn't just writing a book about Michelle by then, I realized, but about Teri too, and two other victims. I wasn't so certain who they were.

But Mary Lou filled me in on the murders of her daughter, Michelle, and her sister, Teri.

Mary Lou Jones is one of the strongest women I know. She is a psychiatric nurse with a Ph.D. who had no reservations about delving into the darkest aspects of the crimes. "No, no," she said softly but firmly, when I expressed my misgivings about asking her some of the questions. "You are writing a book and we want it to be as accurate as possible."

Mary Lou also suggested that I contact some of Michelle's friends. One of them I met without Mary Lou's guidance: Lisa Emmons, who was in the *48 Hours* episode, "Deadly Obsession." Lisa was very straightforward, and contributed to the study of Charlie Brandt. They all did.

And then I met Debbie Knight.

Debbie, of all of Michelle's friends, is possibly the one who carries the most hurt. She was her best friend. She also happens to be a good writer.

She was at Michelle's house two nights before the murder. Debbie believed, and possibly still believes to this day, that she could have prevented the murder of her friend if Charlie had attacked the night that she was there. I tried to convince her otherwise—Charlie would have killed her too. I identify with all these women for different reasons—with Mary Lou, for her wisdom; Lisa, for her honesty; Peggy, for her diplomacy and sweet temper; and Debbie, for her conscience. This last haunts her still, and I wish it would not.

And then I received, via a flash drive, a police report about Sherry Perisho, dubbed "a homeless transient" by the media. She was anything but.

Sherry had a 136 I.Q., read Herman Hesse, and was homeless, apparently, by choice—something akin to "Freedom's just another word for nothing left to lose."

She intrigued me. I reached out to the only person who cared enough about her to keep emailing investigators in Monroe County for the Florida Keys, to find out how her cousin had been murdered. Sherry had been taken and eviscerated by Charlie Brandt.

Through the Monroe County Sheriff's Department and Marilyn Angel, Sherry's cousin, I found out about an autobiography she'd been was writing, which she'd kept in the dinghy she'd made her home. I found a woman I wanted to know. I would have wanted to know Sherry Perisho, and did not get to know her until after she was dead.

Marilyn Angel became a friend. Not an everyday friend, but a friend to whom I sent a Christmas card last year.

I also sent a Christmas card to Special Agent and profiler Leslie D'Ambrosia. She was with me every step of the way, and is a veritable walking encyclopedia of crimes and criminals. She never failed to respond to any question I asked of her, and answered back quite thoroughly and articulately. I could not have done the book without her.

And I also sent a Christmas card to Bill and Mary Lou Jones with a photo of my pets, who give unconditional love, as we all know. I hope it can give them some comfort.

Mary Lou, Michelle's mother, told me she and Bill kept Michelle's cat. They also adopted an injured puppy. They are good people whom I'm glad to know.

I encountered more people as this book progressed: good, kind people who wanted to help.

I went into theatre to explore the human soul in all of its facets. I can now say, after writing about Charlie Brandt, that his is the darkest soul I have ever encountered.

That being said, the good outnumber the bad; the good people, at least in my world, are more powerful, and are getting to be as proactive, or even more so, than the evil ones.

And together, I hope we can keep them from winning. They will not get to win.

Not if any of us have anything to say, or write, about them.

"HIS FRIEND, CHARLIE? A SERIAL KILLER?"

Jim Graves was devastated, and felt somewhat like a fool, when he heard the news about the murders in mid-September of 2004, after all the hurricanes. He was Charlie's good friend. He was Charlie's best man at Charlie and Teri's wedding. Maybe if he told the story over and over from the beginning, it would become transparent, he figured. Just throw it in the cycle at the watering hole and the colors would fade—especially the red.

The colors had been so bright back when he was younger. Each morning had pulled a brand new day from its pocket, instead of this endless folding of moments and tedious hours, piling up for months till he got old.

He was already practically disabled now, from practicing and playing jazz on his guitar so much, and teaching it to others. He had spinal stenosis, four bulging disks and three herniated ones, and cubical tunnel syndrome, which ran from his arm to his hand. He had been a gigging musician, once.

But there was Charlie. Charlie who would never get old or infirm, Charlie who marked the time, Charlie who wouldn't let go. His friend Charlie? A serial killer?

Jim used to go to the bar with Charlie, who'd regaled his buddies with his own tales, over and over till they became more intricate and even murky, splashed with dark hues as he told them. Charlie, who had been his shadow in high school, became the frontman at the joint.

If Charlie went fishing on his boat, he got an overload. When he did his illegal drug runs on that company balloon, it had made him a big stash, enough to buy a $250,000 house—expensive back then—for him

and the wife. It became a running gag inside the bar: "How many, Charlie?"
But before Charlie, there was Angie.

Plate tectonics rocked the planet, wind rocked the water, and Charlie's comment rocked the boat, Charlie's boat, which was about to crash against a dark rogue wave of the soul.

As Charlie and Jim spoke, Jim ranted about the awfulness of his now ex-wife. The misunderstandings, the late nights, the lies, the fuck-yous and the goodbyes; everything predictable, everything kept inside, everything out in the open, everything hidden The ex was Charlie's older sister, Angie. Angie and Jim had met four years earlier, at a concert.

The smell of pot and 1970s idealism had cloaked the audience, beer fueled the human engine, and an alchemist concoction of Quaaludes and Black Beauties kept it running at a high-octane level. Now Daytona Beach legends—then rock stars from Daytona—The Allman Brothers Band had taken the Jacksonville stage in what was to be a magical night for two members in the audience: one that would make them part of a story that would go down in infamy.

Jim and Angie were strangers to one another, but in the midst of being thrown together in a sea of hippie love, they shared a joint, some laughs, a love of rock'n'roll, and, before the night was over, their phone numbers.

After several phone calls, a realization they went to the same school, and a handful of dates, the love-child cherub, the product of expecting the high-school sweetheart myth to become an entitlement, had captured them.

It all ran smoothly for the first four years. What started in high school now led to an apartment, a car, and one individual no longer enjoying the novelty.

In the beginning, the idea of dating a musician was exciting and new to the imaginings of Angie Brandt. The same qualities that have enticed girls since the beginning of rock 'n' roll were the ones that drew her into this union: rebellion, unpredictability, and the potential rock star inside her guitar-slinging significant other.

The turning point for Angie came when Jim transformed from budding guitar player to legitimate gigging musician. At first it had been refreshing. Now it was no longer a kick, but a big, boring pain. Jim strumming the guitar, singing Clapton covers to Angie was now Jim, amplifier cranked to eleven, blasting audio bombs in the faces of packed bars till all hours of the night.

Drunk, smiling, and with money in his pocket, the fact that he was getting paid to have fun wore on Angie who would have to wake up a couple of hours later to work for minimum wage at a menial job as a server.

Angie was reaching her breaking point, and during the last year of their marriage, while Jim was out performing, she had an affair with Dave, the fry cook at the restaurant where she was employed.

When he arrived home one afternoon on his birthday, Jim was given the gift of goodbye. Their Datsun B210, in all of its awkwardly shaped, burnt-orange color, rust-frosted glory was sitting in the driveway, packed to the brim with all of Angie's belongings. She, in matter-of-fact fashion, informed Jim that she was leaving him, and with the pathetic cough of an engine roar, she disappeared down the road.

Donald Withers was friends with both Jim and Charlie since high school. Donald said he'd gotten a call from a couple of friends who'd said they were over at Jim and Angie's, and that Angie had just left Jim. Jim and Angie had been planning to move to St. Thomas because they both wanted to live "eco-friendly." Donald had gone over to the house of another friend, David, when all of a sudden Angie had walked in the door and said, "I just left Jim." Up until this point Donald hadn't even known that Dave and Angie knew one another, but had been told earlier that evening, while hanging out with Dave, that there was a woman he worked with at the restaurant inside the Daytona Beach Airport. That night, as Dave was waiting at the bus stop, she'd approached him and said, "I'm going to go home and leave my husband for you," and sure enough she did exactly that, that evening. Donald said it had been a very weird, coincidental scenario, because he knew all the people involved. The scenario would turn even weirder for Donald much later, when all its participants would do an unusual 180.

However, at the time Jim Graves was absolutely shattered. Through all the booze, gigs, and temptresses, the one thing he had always been was loyal in love.

THE PERFECT REVENGE

Through the years, Jim and Angie's brother Charlie had become pretty tight. While all of Jim's other friends had moved away and settled down, Charlie had always been there to hop in the boat, crack some beers, and go fishing. Desperate, Jim phoned in the Mayday call about his marriage, and Charlie, like the good best friend he was, took his distraught buddy on an escape mission from pain. Destination: the Florida Keys. It was in this land of beautiful, clear oceans, margarita smiles, and warm bright skies that something cold and dark would descend upon the waters.

It was the second day of their trip. They spent the first assaulting their lungs with THC, livers with alcohol, and brain with euphoria. They awoke early to get a head start on their fishing trip. They had been out on the water for a few hours, and Jim could not get Angie out of his head or his heart.

With tears flowing down his face, and anger spewing from his mouth, he lashed out on a diatribe of degrading, spiteful obscenities.

As thoughts of revenge consumed him, the conversation took a horrifying and revealing turn. Charlie sat, silent and understanding for about ten minutes as Jim slandered his sister's name. Then he looked into Jim's face, knife in hand, eyes piercing the soul, and posed the question: "You know what the perfect revenge is, don't you?" Jim didn't know how to respond. Charlie, never breaking eye contact, calculating and cold, continued icily: "Well, the perfect revenge is, you kill somebody and then eat their heart." At that precise instant, a chill froze the orange Florida orb. And from that moment, Jim knew that this man—his friend, his pal, his confidant—was someone he did not know at all.

He told that to correspondent Susan Spencer on the *48 Hours* that aired on CBS on May 25, 2006, two years after Charlie committed one of the most gruesome crimes in Central Florida history. It happened on Tuesday, September 13, 2004. After one look at the scene, three of the responders had gone outside and thrown up.

The question Susan Spencer posed to FDLE Special Agent Leslie D'Ambrosia was what Jim had wondered all of these years: "How many crimes did Charlie Brandt commit?" How many, Charlie? Jim had wanted to ask. But Charlie was no longer here.

THE WIFE WAS
THE LAST TO KNOW

And then, after Angie, there was Nancy. Nancy who Jim was now dating. Nancy who was friends with Teri, and who made him forget Angie. Jim felt like he was in one of those Russian novels where everyone's destinies are intertwined, except in this story it was easier to remember everybody's names.

Charlie had graduated college in Daytona Beach with an electronics degree and immediately got a job with Raytheon, the U.S. defense contractor and industrial corporation with core manufacturing concentrations in weapons. The job was in the Bahamas. Charlie was running, of all things, a drug interdiction operation, which involved the interception of illegal drugs being smuggled into the United States by land, air, or sea. Raytheon had this blimp called "Fat Albert" in the Keys, and Charlie ran it.

In the meantime, Jim had graduated from the School of Music at the University of Miami, was living in South Florida, and was playing with a band. Charlie would fly the guys in and out of West Palm Beach when they had time.

After Angie left, it was back to old times for Jim, hooking up and hanging out and cruising. But Jim's band soon broke up and he moved back to Daytona Beach and got himself an apartment on Seabreeze Avenue, close to the ocean, where he could glue his inner Humpty Dumpty back together again.

One day, Charlie came over to Jim's and told him, "I'm quitting my job in the Bahamas." Jim said, "Well, what are you gonna do? That job's been awesome—you go fishing every day, you say you smoke pot all the time, you got a pocket full of money."

Charlie said, "Well, you're never gonna believe what happened," and he pulled out a fishing rod. "You know what this fishing rod is full of?" Jim shook his head, and Charlie said, "Pure coke."

Charlie told Jim how they all lived in trailers or cottages or some sort of military-like housing that Raytheon provided, and Charlie had been out there, fishing on the flats for bonefish, knee-deep to waist-deep in the water, and bumped up against a duffel bag full of sealed kilograms of uncut cocaine.

At the time Jim was playing guitar all over town and dating Nancy Carney, a very pretty blonde who worked at a radio station. And Charlie, Charlie now had all this money and he moved to Astor, of all places, with a buddy who came down with him from the gig. Astor is a rural area north of Orlando by the St. John's River, a vacation spot for fishing and hunting; and Charlie, he was drinking like a fish and pissing through his money.

Charlie wasn't stupid. He had hidden the duffel bag full of coke in the mangroves back on Andros Island, and just took out little baggies at a time. Initially he had gone back to the trailer and gotten everybody high, even the helicopter pilot.

The helicopter pilot had approached him in private and said, "Where'd you get that?" Charlie had told him, "Well, I bought it in Brown Town," a little settlement there and God knows how many impoverished women he killed there because nobody gives a damn. And the pilot had laughed, "Bullshit, you didn't buy that in Brown Town, there is no fucking way. They'll kill you for five dollars down there. I know somebody who will take it off your hands and give you a ten percent finder's fee."

That turned out to be close to half a million. Jim never got the exact figure, but Charlie's house cost over $250,000 and he paid cash for it.

Jim wasn't religious back then; he just bought into the Kerouak, Gins-berg, and Leary stoner theories of higher power and doors of perception. But now he was a Christian, like folks get when they've been on the edge for so long and need some sort of steering mechanism to take over their lives, and he reflected on Charlie's good fortune. He thought, it just goes to show the devil rewards his own. Here is this guy who murdered his mother and he gets to fucking retire at twenty-eight for finding a bag full of drugs he's supposed to be interdicting.

Then Charlie came home and \asked Jim, "Well, do you know any girls besides your girlfriend? I mean, I've been stuck on that fucking is-land for five, six years, and want to start getting into the scene."

Jim asked his girlfriend Nancy. "Listen, I've got a buddy of mine here who's been living on some island; and um, do you have a girlfriend that's, you know, single? We could go out to the Ocean Deck."

The Ocean Deck is party city, right on the boardwalk in Daytona Beach, right on the ocean, and it has three decks now—for karaoke, for the bands, for dancing, and especially for drinking. It's been here for 40 years, and probably will be for 40 more. No hurricane has ever been able to deface it, or defeat the armies of the night out for a good time.

It was only one deck at that time, but still the place for drinking and dancing and fun in the sun right on "The World's Most Famous Beach." Jim and Charlie met up with Nancy and her girlfriend and roommate at the time, Teri Helfrich, at the Ocean Deck for drinks. Teri had curly blond hair, and was cute and vivacious. She talked up a storm and was funny as hell. Charlie seemed to like her; he was a slow talker and she kind of brought him out. He laughed a lot. They all laughed and drank a lot.

Nancy had moved back to Daytona Beach, after working for Club Med for two years.

"I went to stay with my mom in Daytona Beach for a while, and I met Teri at an aerobics class and we hit it off," she recalls. "So then, when I was looking for an apartment, Teri had a two-bedroom and she said, 'Why don't you move in with me?' So we did!" Nancy Carney never suspected, not even in her wildest imaginings, it would all end so badly.

"Teri was the youngest in our family," her sister Mary Lou recalls, who remembers Teri as a very seemingly lighthearted person. Teri was born in Japan at the Tachikawa Air Force Base while their father was stationed there in the Army Air Corps. He then transitioned to the Air Force.

"She looked like the Sunbeam girl on the bread," said the older sister. "Teri was a fun-loving person and when our Michelle was born," she said referring to their daughter, Bill was in Vietnam on the carrier *Roosevelt*. Michelle and Teri were very close. When Teri graduated from high school she came to live with us. Michelle was in fifth grade."

She was energetic and bubbly, Mary Lou remembered. "We had a brother, Robbie, and he and Teri were very close." Unfortunately, the only boy in a bevy of girls died of leukemia in 1965.

Mary Lou recalled her youngest sister was popular in high school, and had a lot of friends.

Then, Mary Lou went to nursing school in D.C. "Teri was four and a half and didn't remember me when I came back!" Mary Lou said. By then their father had retired from the Air Force in Maryland. He worked for the government after he retired, for the National Oceanographer's Office. When Teri graduated their parents relocated to Gulfport, Mississippi.

Bill Jones married Mary Lou Helfrich in 1965, and Michelle Jones was born in 1966, while her father was in the Navy, in Vietnam, aboard the Carrier *Roosevelt*. Mary Lou moved back home, and Michelle was born at the Andrews Air Force Base in Maryland, "When he got out of the service we set up housekeeping as a family."

After highschool, Teri decided to go to a business college, Jones College, in Winter Park, Florida. She attended the college for one year, and when Bill and Mary Lou moved to Longwood, Florida, Teri lived with them during her first year of college.

However, she decided to move back to Mississippi and ended up going to the University of Southern Mississippi, where she graduated with a degree in business. "She wanted to go into business management," Mary Lou said.

Teri lived with her sister Mary Lou, and her brother-in-law Bill, until 1977, when she graduated from college and went to work at Ivey's Department Store, an upscale department store in Central Florida which is now known as Dillard's. She then transferred to the store in Melbourne, and after one year, she was offered the opportunity to become the store manager at the Ivey's in Daytona Beach in 1984. Every circumstance, every step in her career, was bringing her closer to Charlie Brandt.

Teri then met Nancy Carney, who would introduce her to her future husband and executioner.

Teri was managing all the departments at the Ivey's store in Daytona Beach when she ran into Nancy at an exercise class. The two hit it off, they became friends, and decided to room together in 1984. Nancy worked at a radio station and was dating Jim Graves at the time. Jim and Nancy set up Teri and Charlie on a blind date in 1985, and shortly after dating for a while, the couple moved into an apartment together.

"I remember going over to the apartment for dinner, and to meet Charlie," Mary Lou recalled. Her first impressions of Charlie were that he was laid back and soft-spoken.

"And Teri was an effervescent, outspoken, happy person. They seemed to complement each other." And perhaps Teri was also somewhat gullible.

Around Mother's Day, Mary Lou and Bill went over to Teri and Charlie's place for dinner, and this time they had not only their daughter with them, but also their son, Sean, who was six years younger than Michelle.

Then the two, Charlie and Teri, got married, at Memorial Gardens in Ormond Beach. Jim was the best man and Nancy the maid of honor. They did not invite any family.

For that, Mary Lou stated, Teri had a ready explanation later, when questioned by her sister as to why she and her husband and their parents had not been included. "She said to me, 'If I couldn't have everybody there, I wasn't going to have you there.' That made perfect sense to me at the time, and I did not question it further. But in hindsight I think there would have been some questions asked and Charlie would have been very uncomfortable." What questions would have made Charlie uncomfortable? Questions about his family, perhaps? He told everyone his mother died in a car accident, which was far from the truth.

When Charlie initially came to his best friend Jim, with the news, "I'm going to ask Teri to marry me," Jim said he remembered "flipping out at the time." Jim was twenty-eight years old, and Charlie was twenty-seven. And Jim knew what he knew, and Charlie knew Jim knew. And Jim said, "Uh, well, Charlie, you have to tell her." And Charlie said, "Well, I'm not gonna tell her." And Jim snapped back, "No, you're gonna tell her!" And they went back and forth like kids. After a while Jim tried to put a lid on it, and told Charlie, "Okay, let me put it this way if you're gonna get married and you don't tell her, I'm gonna fucking tell her."

Charlie assured Jim he would tell Teri about that awful night of January 3, 1971, when he had been just thirteen. To this day, nobody knows whether he did tell Teri or not.

Jim knew that Teri had never told Nancy about Charlie, but didn't know if Charlie told Teri at all.

BLOOD RED

After the wedding, Charlie took his profits, the couple moved down to Big Pine Key, and Teri got a job as a receptionist at a dentist's office to make her own money and stay busy. Then she went to work at the Little Palm Island Resort, in the Human Resources department, and Charlie went back to work and ended up running the drug interdiction blimp in the Keys again. Life was good. Charlie and Teri were very lovey-dovey. They would pack each other's lunches because they both said it always tasted better when someone else made your lunch, especially the one you love.

Jim wasn't certain whether Charlie had ever told Teri about the winter in Fort Wayne, Indiana, when Charlie was thirteen, but after Teri dropped the bombshell on him, he was certain he must have. Otherwise, why would she have reacted the way she had?

Five or six years after Charlie and Teri were married, Jim ended up getting a job with Floyd Miles, who was Greg Allman's road manager, to play with a band called Sauce at the grand opening of a place called Hammerhead's, which is two doors down from Sloppy Joe's in Key West. Hammerhead's is not there anymore, but Sloppy Joe still stands, with its Hemingway look-alike contests. It was at an Allman Brothers concert that Jim and Angie had first met. Jim had certainly come full circle.

Jim still had Charlie and Teri's phone number, so he called them up and said, "Look, I'm down here, you know, doing a grand opening for this bar called Hammerhead's on Duvall Street. Why don't y'all come to the club and, watch me play guitar, and we'll hang out and visit and everything?"

As Jim played his guitar, Teri and Charlie walked in and sat. On his first break between sets, Jim went over to their table. Charlie had gone to the bathroom. Teri looked at Jim, with urgency and fear on her face, and said: "I need to talk to you real, real bad. You're not gonna believe what fucking happened and I don't know what to do, I don't know what to do!" She grabbed Jim's wrist.

Jim had been playing really well, and enjoying his newfound local fame. He was in a good mood and full of drink. Charlie, for his part, could tip a few, but was mainly a beer drinker and had to go to the bathroom a lot. And now he was back.

When Jim's next break came up and Charlie headed for the john, Jim went back to the table and asked his friend's wife, "Okay Teri, what's going on?"

She sure showed signs of wear and tear for someone living off the fat of the land, so to speak, and she looked really scared. "I don't know what to do, I don't know what to do!" She looked around, casing the joint, to see where Charlie was.

"Well, just come out with it!" Jim prompted.

"Well, I'm thinking of calling the sheriff on Charlie."

Jim thought, for what? For drugs? Other than Charlie's comment about the heart after Jim and Angie had divorced, Charlie and Teri appeared to Jim like a normal, happily married couple. They had a house built on stilts, like many in the Keys, on account of the storm surge from the hurricanes; and underneath they had a two-car garage. They were on a canal and their boat was parked in the driveway. One had to go upstairs to get to the house, but downstairs they had a little fish-cleaning room with a sink and running water.

Teri went on.

"Well, I came home early from work one night and Charlie was in the fish room. He was all covered in blood, and the whole sink was covered in blood."

Jim offered an explanation he knew too well. "Well, yeah, I mean, you know, it's the fish-cleaning room." Teri's expression showed a mixture of rage and terror. "Well, that's fine and dandy if it's the fish- cleaning room, but there was no fish in the room! And he was all covered in blood!" and Teri was whispering, hoarsely, and her eyes widened and kind of welled up.

Now it was Jim who was looking around for Charlie. "Well, you know, maybe he, he caught some jacks or something, and, just threw 'em in the canal."

Teri was adamant. "No, there were no signs of fish anywhere!" "Maybe Charlie threw the fish away," Jim insisted. And Teri said, "Well, what you don't know is, there was a girl that was murdered, down at the bridge, just a block away or so from the house; they found her in a rowboat, mutilated, and, you know, I'm worried that he might have done it and I've been thinking about calling the sheriff."

Jim was in the middle of this gig, of putting his life back together, of opening this club, and he really didn't want to hear all of this, but Teri kept on. "Well, what do you think I should do, what do you think I should do?" Jim tried to sort out his thoughts.

Jim told Teri: "Here's the deal, Ter. If you call the sheriff, and Charlie has nothing to do with it, your marriage is going to be over. I mean, you can't call the fucking sheriff and say, 'Hey listen, man, this woman died around the corner and I came home and my husband was covered in blood,' so what you have to decide is, like, if it's worth ending your marriage over this kinda far-flung, uh, incident." After all, Charlie did go fishing all the time. It *was* a fish-cleaning room.

Teri did not speak anymore. Jim got up to play. Then Teri and Charlie were gone.

THE SUMMER OF HURRICANES

Hurricane Season extends, officially, from June 1 to November 30, and the Florida peninsula is a magnet for the fiercest storms, jutting out beckoningly between the Atlantic and Caribbean Oceans.

Floridians don't really worry about their 'canes or begin preparations in earnest until late August and the beginning of September. And "conchs," as people in the Keys call themselves for the hard-shelled mollusk indigenous to the islands, hardly worry at all. They don't voluntarily leave their islands, and prefer to ride out the storm. Since semi-apocalyptic Hurricane Andrew in 1992, there was little reason for concern in South Florida. But 2004 became The Summer of Hurricanes, when two severe storms, in a row trained their fury on Central Florida. One of them was Frances. The other one was named Charley.

On September 2, 2004, it was Hurricane Ivan that lashed the Caribbean, killing 68 people. Now its path pointed straight at the Keys.

Monroe County Emergency Management officials began to issue mandatory evacuations.

In Altamonte Springs, near Orlando—the area that had experienced a direct hit from Charley as a Category 1 hurricane—Michelle Jones, Teri Brandt's niece, worried, and kept a close eye on Ivan's track on the local news. Little did she know the lethal combination of rage, fury and desire that was about to strike her in the form of another Charlie, a Charlie she knew.

Michelle, thirty-seven, a successful sales executive with the Golf Channel, which has its headquarters in Orlando, owned a sprawling home with a pool and a Jacuzzi, made cozy and inviting inside by her decorator's touch.

"She was the Accounts Director for Direct Consumer Advertising and

International Sales at the Golf Channel," her proud mother Mary Lou recalls. "For her age, she earned a hefty salary, and was able to afford to buy her first home in 2002. It was a four-bedroom house, a neat little house, thirty-five years old but redone inside, with hardwood floors and butter yellow walls. In her living room she had accents, wall mostly, and cushions on the furniture; reddish and yellow, all warm colors. It had a pool in the backyard and two bathrooms. She loved to shop and accessorize."

Mary Lou Jones remembers her only daughter as "a happy baby, friendly; she was a joy, very intent, and she had a lot of friends. She was in the Brownies, she went to an elementary school in Orlando and a Catholic school for a year, and then we moved to Longwood, Florida. When she finished high school, she worked, when she was old enough to work."

Like every high-school teen who wants to earn her own money, Michelle babysat, but she seemed to manage her money well. When she turned sixteen she worked at some of the stores at the mall. She went to summer school, eagerly, every year, so she could graduate early from high school. And indeed, she graduated when she was sixteen. She went to high school with her best friends, Debbie Wheeler Knight and PeggyAnne Waters Moore. Michelle attended Valencia College for a year, and then all three girls went to the University of Florida in Gainesville in 1984.

But then, her mother explained, "she had a challenge with one of her classes and withdrew from the University of Florida, and decided to finish her Associate's Degree from Valencia College, which she finished in 1988."

Michelle Jones seemed to be as business-driven as her aunt Teri. Once Michelle finished her Associate's Degree she went to work for Channel 35, FOX Network, as Traffic Manager, responsible for communications and for scheduling all the commercial spots that would go on the air. Michelle stayed with FOX until 1994; then, in Saint Petersburg, Florida, she was recruited by one of the major networks, where she remained for six months. In the meantime, Bill and Mary Lou had moved to Pennsylvania, where Mary Lou, who was already a practicing nurse, earned her Doctorate degree. Then Michelle went to work for a marketing firm that did video education promotions, and moved on to the Defalco Advertising Company.

Suzy Hamilton met Michelle Jones at the Golf Channel. Suzy became a steadfast client, and the two young women became close friends.

"I work at a media agency and we did a lot of work with the Golf Channel," Hamilton explained. "She was very loyal and dedicated, and we had a very interesting relationship, because I was working for my clients and she was working for the station."

"We had a thirty-million-dollar account with her, with the Golf Channel—a lot of air, as we call it. And we trusted her implicitly with that kind of money; Michelle was honest to a fault."

Michelle Jones had worked hard to build her career. She was sociable, charming, and persuasive. She asked—she insisted—that her aunt Teri and her husband Charlie wait out the hurricane with her. They'd have fun, she said. They would make dinner and drink wine.

Michelle's aunt and uncle had stayed with her before after Hurricane Georges, which skirted the Keys as a Category 2 and did considerable damage to their home in 1999. Teri and Charlie also had stayed at Michelle's for a week in 2000, while their house was being repaired. There she was, every day for a week in her housecoat, fixing breakfast with "the old lady" Teri. Then she'd get dressed for work and come out of her room smiling, in her high-heeled shoes and her tailored skirts that outlined her round firm bottom. And there she was, every day, for a week, late in the evening, coming back from work, taking her bath, and coming out in her bathrobe with a towel around her head. Now they were there again, going through the same routine.

Charlie and Teri packed a couple of canvas travel bags, hopped in their Subaru Outback, and proceeded to make the trek over the seven-mile bridge connecting the Keys to the Florida mainland.

Hurricane Ivan had reached a dangerous Category 5, but both its strength and path kept fluctuating as Charlie and Teri drove over the bridge on their way to Altamonte Springs. It was the summer of raging, unpredictable natures, and ineluctable, fatal destinies.

The couple arrived at Michelle's house on Saturday, September 11.

From there, Charlie dutifully phoned his father and younger sister Jessica to tell them they had arrived, and to make plans for a family visit.

Since Orlando is about sixty miles, or a little over an hour's drive, from Ormond Beach, where Charlie's father and his youngest sister Jessica resided, Charlie and Teri made plans to see them over the course of the weekend.

They got to Herbert Brandt's house at 2:00 p.m. on Sunday, visited for a while, drank some beers, and then went over to Jessica's for dinner. At Jessica's, Charlie kept telling Teri that it was safe to return to the Keys the next day, and that they ought to begin packing for the trip back. He hadn't wanted to evacuate in the first place, he said. It was all her idea, and Michelle's, he said. They would leave tomorrow, he said. There was a strange insistence, an urgency almost, in his voice.

When he called his older sister Angela from Jessica's house. Angela excused herself for not being able to go to Jessica's, and asked if they could meet the next day. "Sorry, I have plans; we're staying with Michelle," he said. "Maybe next time."

In hindsight, both Charlie's father Herbert and his sister Jessica had noticed that as they said their good-byes, Charlie held each one of them longer and tighter than he ever had.

After the visit, they left to go to back to Michelle's, arriving at her house early in the evening.

They stayed there on Monday too, and Teri was surprised and somewhat miffed, given Charlie's repeated complaints about the pointlessness of evacuating and the need to get back to their home on Big Pine Key. By now the hurricane had bypassed the Keys, veered north into the Gulf of Mexico, and posed a direct hit to Alabama, and now Charlie wanted to stay one more day.

Michelle was beautiful. And she was fun company, too. She and her friends always thought Charlie a little strange; "eccentric" they called him. Michelle thought that he and her aunt Teri made a good pair. Michelle loved her free-spirited aunt who had a mouth on her and reminded her of a hippie girl. Together, Teri and Charlie were adventurous, and Charlie was kind of good-looking, in a sort of goofy, outdoorsy way. He always wore shorts and Hawaiian shirts.

Charlie talked to his friends about Michelle. He called her his "Victoria's Secret," though, of course, not to her face. She wasn't the kind of girl you could kid around with, not like that. "She would have been livid!" recalls her father, Bill Jones, still angry at the notion.

Al Palladino, a co-worker of Charlie's, emphasized time and again that "Charlie was very respectful, to everyone." When Al Palladino was interviewed by lead Detective Rob Hemmert in the Seminole County Sheriff's Office in 2004, after the murders, one of the questions the detective asked him was if Charlie had told him where he and Teri were going during the evacuation.

Al Palladino answered: "On Thursday, he specifically told me, 'If this comes, I'm going up to *Victoria's Secret's* house. This girl has it all! She's intelligent, she has a good job, she has a good home, and she cannot find a good boyfriend. The last guy that she had was divorced. He didn't even have a car! I just don't understand it!' He said she had bad luck. He called her *Victoria's Secret* because the woman was beautiful and looked like someone out of the pages of *Victoria's Secret*. To him, *Victoria's Secret* exemplified beauty." He was quick to clarify that Charlie was never disrespectful to anyone. Notice that he did not refer to the magazine as *Playboy*, Al Palladino pointed out.

Michelle was very close with her mother, Mary Lou, who lived in North Carolina with Michelle's father Bill. Mary Lou Jones also kept close tabs on the hurricane, and knew of Michelle's plans with Teri and Charlie.

By Wednesday, September 15, Mary Lou Jones was worried. She had placed several calls to Michelle, and they had gone directly to her voice mail. It wasn't like her daughter not to return her calls.

Michelle had three close friends, and the three were inseparable. All pretty girls, with good careers and bright futures. The other girls were married, but not Michelle. Michelle had had a four-year relationship with a man who lived with her, but she had broken up with him a year before, on account of his infidelity. Michelle did not seem to have good luck when it came to men.

Mary Lou phoned one of Michelle's friends, Debbie Knight, who lived close by, and asked her to go over to Michelle's house and see if she was there, and if she was okay.

Mary Lou told Debbie that someone from Teri's office had called because Michelle didn't show up at work as expected. Debbie tried to sound casual, but she was starting to sense something strange. "Yeah, I haven't heard from her either and she hasn't answered my messages or emails," the friend answered hesitantly to the mother. Michelle and Debbie were supposed to fly to Vegas later that week for a little getaway, and had been emailing back and forth much more than usual, anticipating the excitement of the trip. This definitely was strange, and not like Michelle, her friend thought.

"Well, would you mind driving over to her house?" Mary Lou asked Debbie, seeking reassurance that her only daughter was all right. She and her husband Bill only had one other child, a boy, Sean, six years younger than Michelle. But she was their baby girl. Debbie immediately replied, "Yes, I will go over right now. I have a house key." She started to walk over to the large wooden bowl on the kitchen counter where she and her husband Pat threw all of their keys. Debbie suddenly felt sick to her stomach. She reached into the bowl to find Michelle's house key. She was heading down the stairs as she quickly told her husband Pat, "Michelle's mom called. She hasn't heard from her either, and wants me to check on her." Pat Knight asked his wife, "Do you want me to go with you?" How unlike him, Debbie thought. Does he think there is something wrong too?

Debbie certainly felt there was something very wrong. But she shrugged off her husband's offer to accompany her because she was in such a hurry. "No, I'm fine," she said, and drove off, with the worst feeling of apprehension in her gut. She phoned their other friend, Lisa Emmons, who also had a key to Michelle's house. All the girls had keys to each other's houses, just in case. Michelle had invited Lisa over for dinner much earlier that night, but Lisa was running late and called Michelle to tell her she would be right over. "Oh, don't bother," Michelle had said on the telephone. "Teri and Charlie have been drinking and arguing, and it isn't very pleasant around here. I'm going to go to my room." Lisa had thought about it for a few seconds, considered going over anyway, and then turned around and gone home. Now, several hours later, Debbie was calling Lisa, and she sounded frantic: "Listen, Mary Lou called me and asked me to check on Michelle and I'm here." Lisa immediately got it. "I'll meet you there," she said.

Debbie was now pulling into the driveway. The first thing she noticed was Teri and Charlie's SUV right there in front of her, in the driveway, blocking the closed garage door, where she assumed Michelle's car was parked. She pulled into the driveway quickly, and stopped in a random spot. As Debbie got out of her car, her mind was flashing terrible scenarios. Maybe they'd died of asphyxiation in the garage inside Michelle's car. Or perhaps they were electrocuted in the Jacuzzi? Ever the careful young mother, Debbie had warned Michelle many times about that Jacuzzi, and now her imagination was getting the better of her. She wanted to run around the back and look in the Jacuzzi, but she was afraid, just terribly afraid, and an inner voice told her *no, don't go back there.* She ran to the front door and grabbed the key she thought fit Michelle's front door, but she was shaking so badly and she couldn't seem to get it to fit into the keyhole. She tried a few times. The door lock would not budge. At this point Debbie didn't even know if she had the right key. So she turned around facing the street, and then turned back around again to the front door. She was desperate now, and worried to death for her best friend. She started banging on the door with both hands and screaming, "Michelle, open the door!" About five or six times she screamed, knocking loudly, "Michelle, open the door!" Then she ran to the family room windows and started banging on the glass. Her heart was racing and the thumping reverberated in her ears. She ran to the right of the house and squeezed herself in between the hedges to get to the bedroom windows. She was banging again at the windows of Michelle's bedroom. Debbie was not screaming anymore. She felt paralyzed with fear. And she did not know why.

Debbie managed to turn helplessly towards the road, looking around the upscale, quiet neighborhood, now drowned in total darkness. She ran to the neighbor's house next door. Debbie started banging on their door and heard herself screaming, "Help! Help! Please someone help me!" No one answered. It was dark inside. No one was home. She then ran across the street, to another house, panting, gasping for air. She spotted someone walking out of the next house, coming out of the garage.

Debbie ran over to the man. "Please, can you help me? My friend is in that house and I think something is wrong, I fear something bad has happened, I haven't spoken to her in days!" She was blurting it all out very rapidly. "My key isn't working and if you could help me break in the front windows to get in the house." The man looked very nervous, but he ran over to his car. Debbie followed him. He grabbed a gun from his car, and a flashlight, and both Debbie and the neighbor ran across the street. The neighbor tried to open Michelle's front door with Debbie's key but to no avail.

"Please! Please, please, please, you have to break a window in the family room!" she pleaded. "We need to get inside the house!" Debbie kept on begging for what seemed like a very long time. The man turned to her and said, "No," cautiously, but firmly. He then proceeded to walk to the back of Michelle's house. Debbie followed the neighbor as he walked toward the garage door and looked through it. Debbie looked through it too and she saw. For a brief second she saw the first horror before the neighbor turned around and pushed her back, so hard she fell to the ground. The man had not wanted Debbie to see, but she saw.

Then the neighbor pulled his cell phone out of his pocket and called 911 to report what Debbie had seen for an instant. "I think there is a man hanging dead in the garage," he told the operator. Then they told the operator something about "multiple deaths." Debbie was certain he said that.

Then Lisa arrived, and so did police officers, who pushed the women back and across the street, and began circling Michelle's house with yellow tape. Then the paramedics arrived, and more police cars and fire trucks. Debbie and Lisa stood in stunned silence, looking at their friend's house from across the street and watching three of the first responders walk out and throw up.

Inside there was, in the parlance of police officers, "a difficult scene," so Seminole County Sheriff Don Eslinger arrived to inspect it as well.

Then a female officer approached both Debbie and Lisa and began asking them questions. She told Debbie, "I need you to describe Michelle to me." Debbie was then certain of what she'd known all along, that something was terribly wrong inside that house, something evil, the depths of which she didn't even dare fathom.

Once she was told outright about the murders of Teri and Michelle, she called Bill Jones in North Carolina and uttered the dreaded words: "Michelle is dead. Michelle is dead." Debbie repeated the phrase to Michelle's father about five times, like a tearful mantra, as she heard the deafening silence on the other side.

Inside, the detectives and Sheriff Eslinger found a crime scene filled with horror and depravity. Teri Brandt was slumped over on a living-room couch, covered in blood. She had been stabbed seven times.

Michelle, or what was left of her, was in her bedroom, lying on her bed. She had been stabbed once in the chest, decapitated, and her head was placed beside her body, as if to view all of the carnage. Her heart was cut out and her breasts had been severed, and also placed on the bed. Her intestines were deposited in the trash bin in the bedroom.

Detectives Rob Hemmert and Bob Jaynes had never encountered anything like this.

"It was absolutely stomach-turning; it was horrific," recalls Steve Olson, a Seminole County sheriff's spokesperson. "It was rough, even for some of the more seasoned people."

And strewn all over the bedroom floor, as if with grim irony, were Michelle's panties and bras, all shredded with the same knife. The brand: *Victoria's Secret.*

This almost raises the question: why did Charlie refer to Michelle as *"Victoria's Secret?"* Did he know she wore that brand of underwear, or was it just on account of the beautiful models?

But then, why did he order and keep *Victoria's Secret* catalogues? And when did he start doing this? After he and Teri stayed at Michelle's house while their home on Big Pine Key was being repaired? Had he rummaged through her drawers? Even more perversely, had he worn the underwear, like disgraced Canadian Air Force Colonel Russell Williams?

Detectives Hemmert and Jaynes concluded that, after stabbing his wife Teri with one of Michelle's kitchen knives, Charlie Brandt had spent a long time with Michelle Jones. The investigators spent two days examining and inventorying Michelle's house, the beautiful Florida home she'd so carefully decorated, now a house of death.

When Hemmert and Jaynes checked the FBI database, the MO and signature of the killings matched exactly that of Sherry Perisho in Big Pine Key, the homeless former beauty queen who was found about a thousand yards from Charlie and Teri's house.

Special Agents Leslie D'Ambrosia and Sergeant Dennis Haley had been dispatched on hurricane detail when they were called to the crime scene of the Brandt/Jones murders. After they were briefed on the details of those crimes, Haley said he and D'Ambrosia looked at each other and exclaimed, almost in unison: "That's the guy who did Perisho!" Sherry Perisho had been killed and eviscerated under the Big Pine Key Bridge, a few blocks away from the Brandt home, in 1989.

There had also been another similar crime in Miami-Dade County, plus twenty-six others with the same ritualistic characteristics. The investigators then proceeded to the garage. There was Charlie.

Apparently, after he was done with Michelle, he had showered changed into clean clothes—a white polo shirt and blue shorts. He then found a long, white bed sheet, got a metal stepladder from the garage, and hung himself by the neck from the rafters.

Then Angela Brandt came forth with the story, the secret the family had so carefully guarded since 1971, about the winter of Charlie.

Angela told Detective Rob Hemmert, during that interview, that in the house in Fort Wayne, Indiana, she'd lived with her parents, Ilse and Herbert, and her two little sisters, Melanie and Jessica.

"It was the day after Melanie's second birthday, and Jessica was three but almost four. I was fifteen."

It was 9:00 or 10:00 p.m., she said. "We had just gotten a color TV. We were all sitting around watching *The FBI*. I'd gotten a book like I always did before I went to sleep. My mom was reading *Time Magazine*."

Angela said she remembered her two little sisters' room was "in the bedroom right behind me." She seemed to also recall her mom was thirty-seven, and her dad was two years older.

"I was in my bedroom reading, and I heard really loud noises, which I perceived to be firecrackers," Angela stated. "So I started pulling my covers down to find out what it was, and then I heard, 'Charlie, no!' or 'Charlie, don't!' and I heard my mom scream, and then say, 'Angela, call the police.' So like I said, I was pulling the covers off my bed, and getting out of the bed. And this had to be less than a minute later. And Charlie comes into my room brandishing a gun, a handgun. I didn't realize what it really was, until he aimed it at me, and he pulled the trigger!" Angela related it almost casually, but was obviously still surprised by her brother's action. "I could hear it click," she almost whispered now. "I guess when he realized the gun didn't have any more bullets, that must be when he threw it on the floor. I guess I was lucid enough to kick it under the bed. I didn't even know the gun didn't have any more bullets. And that's when a physical altercation ensued. I imagine, I think, he struck me! I had blood, and... bruises! And I fought back! This is the only physical altercation I've ever been in my life, and I guess I won because I'm here to tell about it!" she said, becoming more agitated now. "I was only fifteen and I was still trying to assimilate what was going on and I was still trying to get away from him; he was very strong! I really don't know what happened in the next five or six seconds; I was laying here at the foot of my bed, and he was sitting on me, and he was strangling me. I don't think that I got him off of me physically. I *saw* the weird look on his face, the madness, the glazed-over look, disappear. I could see his face, and he looked more like himself and he said, 'What did I do?' and I said, 'I don't know, but I think you shot Dad. And he said, 'Oh, I did?' And I said, 'I don't know but get off me so we can figure it out!' And he did, he got off of me. If I did anything wrong when I was fifteen you'll have to forgive me. I was trying to save my life."

Her thoughts got confused at this point, and then she remembered again. "He got off of me. He said, 'What are we going to do?' I said, 'I don't know because I don't know what you've done!' I said, 'I think you've killed or done something to Mom and Dad; I think we ought to go downstairs.' And the only reason I wanted to go downstairs was because at the bottom of the stairs was the door, to get out! So I decided I'd make up a story. It was the seventies, so I said, 'We'll run away to a hippie commune!' And he said, 'Oh! Well, okay!' But I had to get him away from me so I could turn the knob and get outside, because my dad was all about bolting the door, and I hadn't seen my mom and dad. But I do remember one bizarre thing. This was in Indiana; it was cold. And we hacked wood, we had two fireplaces, and my dad remembers me telling him this the other day. There was a bucket and there was an axe. Apparently when you live up north you keep your axe in the water, something about the shrinking of the wood. I remember walking by that axe, and turning around and going, 'Let's go in another room!' because I didn't want him to see the axe.

Charlie was gonna pick it up and hack me to death!"

Angela now began to talk very, very rapidly. "And I don't remember what gibberish I was telling him, something about running away! And I remember telling him, 'It's very cold outside. You need to go upstairs and get a blanket for Melanie and Jessica,' because of course I was going to take them with me! I was fifteen, I couldn't even drive! Where were we going to go? I just wanted to get out of the house. And he bought it. And he began to go upstairs but backwards. And he was saying, 'Angie, if I go up here you're not going to leave me, are you?'" And now Angie burst into tears, into frightening and terrifying tears. "And of course I said no! And as soon as I knew he was far enough away, I ran! Have you ever seen '*The Texas Chainsaw Massacre?*' I saw it once in my life, and I could never see it again! You remember the girl screaming, the girl running down the road screaming? That was me! I was just a little girl, and I was running through the snow in my bloody and torn nightgown, screaming!"

Angela ran to neighbors' houses; she knocked on two doors and there was no one there. Then she ran to the next house, and by that time Charlie was outside, and the whole time, Angie heard him screaming, "Angie, you promised me you wouldn't leave me! You promised you wouldn't leave me!" And now Angela was sobbing again as she said, "And I did!" Detective Rob Hemmert tried to console her, telling her under the circumstances it was understandable. But she went on.

She said she'd burst into the neighbors' house without knocking; they were playing cards, and she was screaming, "I think Charlie killed my mom and dad!" and the next thing, all the men went across the street "because all this time, unbeknownst to me, my father had picked his guts off the bathroom floor, crawled to the phone and called the operator. So all these officers came, and they picked up Jessica. She was all bundled up, and someone said, 'I'm so sorry honey, but your mom is dead,' and then someone picked up Melanie. So there I was, sitting there, trying to understand what was going on."

Then an officer took her back to her house and told her to put her clothes on and her overcoat on. They picked up the gun from under the bed. "I remember they searched me. But then it was fine; I didn't have anything on me. I wanted to be a hippie; I had Beatles posters all over my walls. Then we went to the police station, where I told them what I knew. I don't remember if at this point I had any family members with me. I didn't know if my dad was still alive; I knew that my mom was dead. I said, 'Before you take me to the hospital I have to see my brother.' And they said no. And they said, 'It's not normal procedure.' And I said, 'Well, it's not a normal night.' And they brought him to me. And he was all chained up. And he just looked up at me, and he immediately started crying, and he said he was so sorry, and I said, 'I know.' And we both started crying. And I had no animosity towards him whatsoever."

After that, Angie talked about her father's hospital stay, and about their mother's funeral, and how the family came home from Germany.

Her father wanted to take everything out of the house; he took a year's absence from work, and they moved to Florida, to Ormond Beach. "To people who came to Florida from Berlin, this was Paradise."

At this point, Detective Hemmert asked Angie if she remembered anything her father had told her that night. "He sat on the toilet and wept, and said, 'I'm nothing without my wife.' He never had counseling; he didn't believe in counseling."

Now that Angie was somewhat calmer and well into the story, Hemmert asked her if she remembered how her parents were shot.

And now her demeanor was more casual, even somewhat upbeat.

"This is as I remember. My mother was in the bathtub reading *Time Magazine* and catching up on the mail; my father was shaving, getting ready to work the next day. And apparently my brother shot my dad, and I don't remember who was shot three times and who was shot twice. The chamber held nine bullets and there were only five in there. And I only learned this the other night. My father was very frugal, and he said if the gun was full, it compressed the spring or something. My father told me how he pulled the drain out of the bathtub. He told me how he pulled his body together and crawled to the phone, and then he went unconscious. I know he was shot in the abdomen, and I think my mom was shot in the heart. I don't know if it went to her abdomen."

While Charlie was in jail, his father had milk delivered to him, because the inmates were only allowed coffee and water. "I was ill! I cried for five months in a row! I was sedated to sleep. But the first thing my father said to me was, 'Your mother…' and I said, 'She's dead, Daddy.' And he said, 'What about your brother?' And I said, 'He's in jail.' And he said, 'Oh the poor kid, he must have snapped!' Charlie had a Grand Jury but he was not convicted. From what I know, my brother was in jail for five or six months; he went into the state mental hospital. And… can a state or a town make you leave? Because I was under the impression he could no longer reside in the community." Detective Hemmert told Angie that this varied from state to state but that it probably applied.

From the Indiana State Mental Hospital Charlie went to live with his father in his new apartment in Fort Wayne.

Shortly after that, they moved to Florida, to Ormond Beach. "I could have been a lawyer, too; believe me, I'm no idiot," Angie said disparagingly. "This has basically pretty much ruined my life, okay? I went from a straight A and B Honor Roll student to D's and F's. When I was sixteen years old I quit high school to take care of Melanie and Jessica. I got a GED, and got a job."

Hemmert wanted to know, "Prior to this happening on January 3rd of 1979, was there anything you saw, growing up with Charlie? Did you see something in Charlie that would have given any indication that he could…"

Angela was quick to answer, "No—my dad and I have talked about this for thirty years. I didn't know people did things like that! I thought it only happened in crime novels I wasn't allowed to read."

The detective asked if Charlie had said anything to her while he was trying to strangle her. She said he hadn't. "It was all basically like a nightmare."

Angela remembered when Charlie was ten or eleven, when it was dinnertime, he would crawl in her bed. "And he would say, 'There are monsters in my room!' There were never any monsters in my room!"

Dennis Rader, "the BTK Killer," (for Bind, Torture and Kill) said monsters were driving him to commit the murders that rattled Kansas City for three decades. But then, in Charlie's case, it might have just been the imaginings of a lonely child.

The detective asked what their relationship was like when they became adults. "At first, my boyfriend and I lived with Charlie. Then I stayed away from him, but I know why—because once I was a mom, I didn't want him near my children. I let myself at the time think that we had just grown apart. But now I think it was because as I gained more wisdom, and I'm almost fifty now, subconsciously I was trying to protect my kids from what may or may not be. I don't know why I didn't see him that much anymore."

Hemmert wanted to know if there were any more visits. "I thought to myself, he has a house in the Keys; he has a boat! Why don't I go there?" she almost laughed. I know exactly why deep in my soul. I thought, I didn't want to sleep in his house; he tried to kill me! Intellectually I thought, no. In my heart, there were questions. The first night he ever stayed in the Fort Wayne apartment with us, I never slept a wink. I had that door locked; I had whatever jammed under that door. But in the morning I was sociable with him, and we made breakfast. I guess I thought he only killed at night!"

The detective asked if they had spoken on the phone since.

"Yes, that Sunday!" Angela meant right before the murders.

"Only because of the evacuations! I came home from work and there was a message from Jess, from Jessica! It said, 'I'm going to the store now to make lasagna, why don't you come?' I wasn't going to go over there at six-thirty at night. But what I did say to my brother was, 'I can't come tonight, but what about tomorrow night?' He said, 'No, we're staying at Michelle's.' But I didn't know who Michelle was."

Detective Hemmert wanted to know if their father was a strict disciplinarian, if there were any family disputes. "He was very strict but he never beat us or anything."

"Was he strict across the board with each child?" Hemmert then wanted to know.

"He expected Charlie to be manly," Angela said.

"And was he?" Hemmert asked.

"No," Angela replied, explaining that Charlie was bullied in school. And then, Charlie went to work in Andros Island.

Detective Hemmert wanted to ask about his relationship with Teri, and she said they always appeared very loving.

"Let me ask you this: ever since you found out what Charlie did, what has the discussion been like with your dad?"

She said her father called her on Wednesday in the middle of the night and said, 'Angela, I have very bad news. You know, your brother and Teri have been missing for a couple of days. And where Teri's niece lives, in that house, they found two bodies. And in my mind immediately I thought, poor Charlie, to have such a violent end after all he's been through in his life. And my dad said, 'But Charlie was killed also.' And then I said, 'Really? But there are evacuations all over.' And he said, 'I just feel it. It just couldn't be, not after all this time.'"

Angela finally asked Detective Hemmert: "You *are* going to give us some kind of closure, aren't you? Even though the perpetrator is dead, you want to give some closure to the family, don't you?"

"I have to," Hemmert said with finality.

THE WINTER OF CHARLIE

These eyes will deceive you, they will destroy you. They will take from you, your innocence, your pride, and eventually, your soul. These eyes do not see what you and I see. Behind these eyes one finds only blackness, the absence of light. These are the eyes of a psychopath.

– Dr. Samuel Loomis, *Halloween*

Jim was the one who introduced Teri to Charlie.

And back when Jim and Angie were shacked up, Angie told him the story, the story about that night, that Sunday in January 1971.

The summer of 1973, Jim was looking forward to being a senior in high school. He and Angela were sixteen, and Charlie was fifteen.

"I live in the Ghetto-by-the-Sea," Jim told his friends, referring to Cypress Circle in Ormond Beach. And his friends were warning him about "the pregnant story." They said, "You know, one of these days you're gonna come home and she's gonna be bawling and say, 'I have something to tell you, and it'll be the 'I'm pregnant' story.'"

One day, Jim came home and there she was, Angie, crying on the couch.

He thought to himself, "Oh man, here it comes, and I don't even know what my answer is gonna be. I just thought my friends were full of shit."

Angie just looked up at him and said, "I gotta tell you something."

It was Sunday January 3, 1973 and Three Dog Night's "Joy to the World" dominated the airwaves. And that's when Angie told Jim about the winter of Charlie.

Jim had met Charlie only a few months before, when the Brandts moved to Ormond Beach from Fort Wayne. Jim met the brother through Angie, and of course when he started to meet her family and relatives, he and Charlie became friends.

Angie went off to work and left Jim just sitting there, with no outlet other than to crack a beer. He couldn't tell any of his friends this! He couldn't believe it—in fact, he was just going to blow it off it was so far-fetched. He could have handled the pregnant story from Angie, but the pregnant mother in the bathtub, and Charlie?

Jim was growing more agitated as he lit up a joint and did more damage to the six-pack in the fridge. "C'mon! I met her brother and he's completely fucking normal!"

On Thanksgiving Day, Jim and Angie decided to go to her father's house and his parents' house, since their two families lived in town.

They decided to first visit her father in Ormond-by-the-Sea, the furthest point south from Ormond Beach, which was adjacent to Daytona Beach, and part of Volusia County.

Herbert Brandt was mowing the lawn, and he was shirtless. Jim spotted the bullet scars in the man's back, since Charlie had not only killed his pregnant mother, but shot his father, tried to choke his sister, and left the two little ones, his younger sisters, alone.

Jim felt sick, like he'd just chugged a twelve-pack of warm ones and was about to vomit. He decided to go back to his parents' house later that night. How could he deal with this situation he asked them? Well, they both kind of said, especially his mother, if you like him, and he is a good friend, and if God has forgiven him, you can too.

But Jim was not satisfied. He sat Angie down and said, haltingly, "You know...I saw your father today." And she replied, "Uh, yeah." He was firm. "You know, you know if we're going to continue this relationship..."

She knew what he meant. He wanted the entire story.

They were full-blooded Germans, the Brandts, straight out of Berlin. Angie's grandfather on her mother's side had been in both World Wars. Angie's father had been in a Hitler Youth camp during World War II. "You mean, where they brainwash the kids to believe that Aryan Nation stuff?" Jim said. "Well, I don't know how old he was, but he was in one of those camps." Angie looked down.

Charlie and Angie's parents, immigrated to America. Herbert Brandt got an engineering job at International Harvester in Fort Wayne, Indiana, and the two began raising a family.

Angie was born first, and then Charlie.

Charlie was an introverted, shy and chubby kid, who had no friends in school and got picked on all the time. Herbert was probably not very pleased that his only son wasn't living up to the expectations of the Aryan Nation.

But they took vacations back then, in the sixties, when folks actually took family vacations every year, and they came down to Florida when Charlie was twelve or thirteen at the time. They stayed at the Coral Sands in Ormond-by-the-Sea, and the whole time Daddy was mulling around trying to decide what to do with his sissy kid, and decided to take him hunting.

This was west of I-95 before the building boom, and it was all swamp and hammocks. And it turns out the only friend Charlie really had was the family dog, a beagle, and they took the dog with them, he and his dad.

The story Jim heard was that Herbert shot the dog. Jim was thinking maybe Charlie shot the dog; maybe the rage boiled over that early, his way of controlling something, anything. Herbert said he didn't mean to shoot the dog, just to scare him out of the bushes so he would come home with them.

When the vacation was over, they went back up to Fort Wayne. The really bad thing happened a week after they got back home from vacation.

Charlie was an introvert. His dad had shot his best friend, maybe. That's the story anyway; that the dad shot the dog, and maybe that's what set him off. Maybe the father wanted to make a man out of Charlie and teach him a lesson. Who knows what happened out there in the swamp? But the dog got shot.

Anyway, they were back home in Indiana, and everyone remembers the date now, like that other date in 2004, when Hurricane Ivan was threatening the Florida Keys.

On Sunday, January 3, 1971, there was an ice storm in Fort Wayne, Indiana. It was after dinner, after dark, and Charlie was sitting at the kitchen table. Charlie's mother Ilse chided the boy for not having his homework finished, and both father and mother went upstairs to the bathroom, like Angie told Detective Rob Hemmert.

The real sequence of events that Angie did not see was culled from investigators and newspaper accounts.

The mother was reading *Time Magazine* and the father was shaving when, suddenly, the silence was punctured by the sound of gunshots.

Herbert screamed, "Charlie, stop!" and Charlie fired several times at his mother, who slumped down in the bathtub, dead. She was eight months pregnant.

Then he went after his sister, Angie. The gun jammed and he tried to strangle her. Angie fought him as hard as she could, hitting him and scratching him and pleading, "Charlie, I love you! I love you!" She asked him to go upstairs, to the linen closet, to get warm blankets for her little sisters, Melanie and Jessica. She told Charlie they would run away, but she was biding her time until she could get to the door, open the bolt, and run out. Charlie was doing as his sister told him, but she noticed, with a fear that was colder than the weather outside, that he was walking backwards. "You're not going to leave me alone, are you?" he said, and the glazed, manic expression on his face dissipated. "No, of course not!" she said. But she did. And she ran, ran for her life, ran in fear of her own brother. But this fear of abandonment would surface again later throughout Charlie's life.

It was a year later, when Charlie was freshly released from the asylum, that the doctors explained there was no threat that he would ever act out again. Little did they, or his possible twenty-six future victims, know the fury that had begun in the core of the thirteen-year-old boy. A boy who should have carried a tombstone as a nametag. A boy who had discovered the surge of power that comes from plunging a knife into a beating heart. A boy who was a reaper from the Midwest encased in the confines of flesh, bone, and a convincing smile that would have the world welcoming him as their friend Charlie. A boy they described as compassionate, friendly, and willing to do anything for anyone. The truth was this: He was a son, brother, husband, and friend. But, also a child, an adult, and a depraved horror story that took forty-seven years to end.

Evil is unspectacular and always human,
And shares our bed and eats at our own table.
— W. H. Auden

A HUMAN HEAD INSIDE
A PAINT CAN

Jim thought back to the time when he was studying music at a state university and Charlie decided to go to Daytona Beach Community College.

It was the spring of 1977, and hotter than a volcanic cavern. Fresh off the lukewarm winter winds of the previous months, Floridians squirmed with anticipation. The youth, conditioned through this climate, understand that it is now only a matter of weeks before they can surf the waves with beet-red burnt skin and the smell of late sunscreen. On the other hand, the elderly are beaming with excitement that the bone-chilling sixty-five-degree weather of the "cold season" has now passed and the humid blanket will soon be heating their thinned blood through its hair-dryer breeze. This is the transition and the preparation period. It will soon be summer.

In the midst of this changing of the seasonal guard, in a calm white Daytona Beach neighborhood there was a quaint, pink house. The owner, Mrs. Graves, had had a forgive-to-be-forgiven philosophy ingrained in her by a strong religious upbringing. She knew of her son Jim's friend Charlie's past atrocities. She had heard the stories from Jim. However, she decided that if doctors agreed and the Lord absolved Charlie, she did not have the right to turn someone out on the street. With her son off to FAU (Florida Atlantic University), welcoming her son's best friend Charlie into her home seemed like the appropriate thing to do.

Although his childhood goal had been to become a pilot, Embry Riddle Aeronautical College would not accept Charlie; nobody knew why. This, coupled with the fact that Charlie's roommate was going to be moving on from their current dwelling, left the young man in need of a place to reside while finishing his new plan for the future: earning a degree in Electronics from Daytona Beach Community College. Jim, having had a successful stint at FAU, saw the upcoming spring break on the horizon as a perfect time to not only take a break from the grueling hours of guitar practice and study, now accountable for his many ailments, but also a perfect time to visit his now ailing mother while also catching up with his best friend Charlie. Mrs. Graves planned to have the boys over for dinner, and figured it would give them all a chance to reconnect, laugh, and enjoy the comforts of a mother's home-cooked meal.

The dinner conversation went as most dinner conversations go—well, kind of. Throughout the meal and the beers, the men explained how they were doing in their classes, their like for some professors and extreme distaste for others, and how and what they planned to do when their collegiate ride came to its inevitable end. Jim discussed his plan to continue live gigging while supplementing his income by giving private teaching lessons for other up-and-comers. Charlie, in Charlie-like fashion, had decided he would see what opportunities came his way.

As both men became tired of talking about the same topic, Mrs. Graves took note and turned the conversation towards the news. Reclusive by nature, but polite and liked by those who knew her, Mrs. Graves explained how she had heard from a neighbor about a local news story stating that a thirteen-year-old girl's head had been found inside of a paint can in the city of Astor. At that moment, Charlie burst into absolutely maniacal laughter. Almost in synchronicity, Jim's head went spinning as his brain was thrust into the violent outer bands surrounding a storm of vicious thoughts:

BOOM! BOOM! BOOM!

"Charlie, stop!"

A grown man's back riddled with bullets behind a bathroom door.

BOOM! BOOM! BOOM!

A thirty-seven-year-old mother carrying an eight-month-old life that would never see another day, past betrayal, lying limply in shattered porcelain.

The sound of a jammed gun being thrown onto a bedroom floor.

"Charlie, I love you! I love you!" through the gasp and gurgles of the dying mother, a sister's plea. The glazed eyes of a thirteen-year-old staring back.

"You're not going to leave me alone, are you?" he asks her.

"HELP! HELP!" A sister desperately runs from her own brother, and bangs on the neighbors' doors.

A boat out in the warm waters of the Florida Keys. Two men, two friends, one cursing his former wife, maligning her to her own brother. Her brother, his friend, holds a knife in his hands. And then the glazed stare again: "Well, the perfect revenge is, you kill somebody and then eat their heart."

Jim snapped out of the daydream of ominous memories and hints of future possibilities, coming to within the confines of his cold, now goosebump-riddled skin. Clammy and with a racing heart, he wasn't sure what to do next. The only thing he was sure of was that Charlie's sadistic laugh was still serenading the dinner table.

After his stay at Jim's mother's house, Charlie moved in with his friends, Jim "Jimbo" Elbers and Lonie Weiner, and they all lived on San Juan Avenue in a huge house in Daytona Beach. They described themselves as a happy little family of hippies and they all lived upstairs in the three bedrooms, turned the bathroom into a fish room for storage, and built furniture together.

Lonie remembered that Jim Graves had told them about the dinner when Charlie busted out laughing about the head in the paint can, and about how creeped out he was, but they'd all brushed it off as, "Oh, that's just Charlie." Lonie suspected that maybe that evening had been the reason why Charlie had had to move out of Jim's mom's house. Maybe, based upon Jim's mom's knowledge of Charlie's past, plus Jim's own suspicions, Jim had suggested Charlie move out of his mom's house, and into Lonie and Jimbo's.

Charlie worked at Bahama Joe's for a while, and then worked as a maintenance man at a condominium complex while he was attending Daytona Beach Community College and living with Lonie and Jimbo.

"Charlie loved working there at the condo complex, because he could leave school early and head out through Tomoka and fish for a while," Lonie remembered. "And then Tomoka Road took him right to his job. Every day he could fish in between school and work, alone."

Lonie stated that Charlie would bring home fish that he caught every night for dinner. She never remembered Charlie having a girlfriend.

"He was sweet; he was helpful, never strange, cruel, abusive," Lonie said. "He was just gone fishing a lot. He would be up at like 6:00 a.m., be off to school, come home, get his fishing stuff, get in his Volkswagen, and leave."

Lonie did remember that Charlie did a lot of fishing in Osteen. "In fact, he went to Osteen quite a bit," she said.

Osteen was where Carol Lynn Sullivan was seen for the last time, at her bus stop, waiting to go to her junior high school.

ANDROS ISLAND

J im did not hear anything from anyone until he found out what had happened on Tuesday, September 13, 2004. He placed a call to the Florida Department of Law Enforcement (FDLE) and said, "I don't know why you people haven't called me, but I think you really need to talk to me." Jim was carrying two terrible burdens now. He was not absolutely certain Teri had known about Charlie when he was thirteen. It might have saved her life, and Michelle's, if she had. And he had not paid attention to Teri's story about Charlie, all bloody in the fish room. That might have saved them too, and some others.

Jim proceeded to tell the FDLE investigators the entire story about the club on Duvall Street in Key West, and how Teri had come to him with the fish room story. The investigators concluded that the timeline for that particular crime was accurate, as well the signature. It was clear Teri was right, that Charlie had done it.

The officers asked Jim about the different places where Charlie lived. He said, "You know, over there in the Bahamas he was living on that small island with you know, where there was this little black town and everything. If anybody went missing over there or anything, nobody would really give a shit, you know, so who knows?"

There was some irony to Charlie arriving in the Bahamas, according to Donald Withers, who visited Charlie there. "The drug culture in Daytona Beach at that time, in the late 1970's, was through the roof," Donald Withers observed.

Daytona Beach was a major party city back then, and Charlie had told his friend Donald it was going be nice to go somewhere to get away from all of that for a while. "Well, the day after Charlie was dropped off by helicopter at Alltech Site 3 at Big Wood Key in the Bahamas, where he was to work, all of a sudden a big bale of cocaine, the one Charlie would later sell, washed up on the shore," his friend Donald Withers said. Donald Withers also remembered that, thirty yards west of the Alltech site on Andros Island, Charlie came across about four hundred yards of bales of coke under cargo netting. "The area was about four to five hundred yards long, and about a hundred yards deep. This meant thousands and thousands of bales! Whoever was trafficking in the coke would bring it to that site for drop-off and then the speedboats would pull up every night and pick up their load to deliver it to the United States. So if Charlie thought he would get away from the Florida drug culture, and kind of use the trip as a form of rehab, he ended up right in the middle of the monster. But perhaps he wanted it that way, who knows?"

Charlie told Donald that within the first four or five days he was there, they were snorting lines of coke off the radar screens that they were supposed to be using to find the planes the DEA had under surveillance.

"As I know, Charlie was a recreational drug user who was always very good about not letting himself get out of hand, and maintaining control," Donald said.

Donald and two friends from New Smyrna Beach, near Daytona Beach, took a twenty-two foot sailboat down to Andros Island on vacation and stayed on Alltech Site 3 for about three weeks with Charlie in one of the trailers Raytheon provided. There were only about six to eight people on that base with Charlie, Donald said. Charlie had not yet begun working the blimp and was strictly working the drug radars at that time. He was working the blimp at the time when he moved to Big Pine Key with Teri. With some early coke money he made while working on Tech Site 3, Charlie bought an eighteen-foot outboard boat.

"Charlie would make trips in and out of the United States to make coke-selling runs, while working at Alltech Site 3," Donald said. The friend believes that Charlie would catch trips back into the United States by Alltech planes going back and forth.

"After Charlie moved to Big Pine Key, we pretty much lost contact with one another," Donald Withers said. Withers stated he had gone to the Keys several times on vacation, and one time he went to Charlie's house to say hello as he was passing by, but Charlie wasn't home.

The investigators said that during the times Charlie traveled to Miami, the police found torsos and body parts. So they began to visit the scenes and found the same MO and signatures during the same time periods.

Jim also told the investigators about the head in the paint can, the head of the thirteen-year-old girl found on September 20, 1978 in Osteen, where his former roommate, Lonie Weiner, said Charlie used to go fishing all the time.

He also told them he and Charlie were at Jim's mother's house when they found out, and about Charlie's reaction, and the look on his mother's face. But they never did tie him to that crime. To this day, Jim still thought Charlie had killed her, that he'd killed that little girl over in Astor, just from the way his mom reacted and everything.

For his part, and in another strange coincidence, Donald Withers, Charlie and Jim's high-school friend who was had witnessed Angie leaving Jim, said that when he heard about the head in the paint can story, and for reasons he couldn't explain, the hairs on the back of his neck stood up. "I just got this feeling in my gut," the now-successful businessman said.

After pondering the incident for a long while, Donald Withers said he remembered a kind of strange occurrence one night. He remembered he and Charlie used to frequent P's Bar, now a nightclub on International Speedway Boulevard, where the Daytona 500 takes place. The friends stayed there drinking until the place closed, and usually, after a hard night of drinking, they crashed at whoever's home was the closest to the place. Donald Withers recalled that one night, about three or four in the morning, he heard Charlie get up and leave without saying a word, which he found odd. For one thing, Charlie never did that and also, they had a fishing trip planned for the next morning.

The next day when Donald woke up, there was bad weather, so he thought maybe Charlie had somehow heard something about that and decided to go home. Donald brushed it off and never thought to question Charlie about it. Donald Withers does not remember the timeline for that incident, but added that, for some reason, when he heard the paint can story, that night that Charlie took off with no explanation, popped into his head.

Donald also made mention of the "glazed look" that would come over his friend at times, which he attributed to a kind of drifting off. "He would just get that kind of lost, glazed look, and I would have to say, 'Hey man, come back!' to make him snap out of it."

As the officers were leaving Jim Graves's apartment, Jim said to one of them: "Look, uh, how could I know this guy my whole life and this shit, uh, woosh! Over my head. You know what I mean?" One officer responded: "If your mind doesn't work like the mind of a psychopath, sociopath, serial killer, that's how you miss it. Because if you're not like-minded you don't make the connection."

Charlie Brandt, serial killer. Charlie? His friend, Charlie?

Nobody had suspected: not Michelle's best friends, who knew Charlie, not Michelle's mother Mary Lou, Teri's sister. And not Jim. Especially not his fishing buddy, Donald Withers.

Donald said he never heard any more about or from Charlie until their thirty-year high-school reunion. A couple of Donald's friends went to the reunion and came back and told Donald they heard that Charlie had killed his wife and hung himself. "I was shocked," Donald said. "I never even remotely saw that side of Charlie."

After the CBS *48 Hours* segment "Deadly Obsession" aired, Donald said Dave called Jim and told him he was furious that they had done the special and that the program was "demonizing" Charlie. Dave was also furious because it put his then-recently divorced wife through hell, having it all back in the spotlight.

"They (Angie and Dave) just didn't want to believe anything more could have happened other than Charlie's past with the mom," Donald Withers said. "They said it was finger-pointing and just cops trying to close cold cases and so forth. They just did not want to believe it."

This does not jell with Angie's voluntary interview with Detective Rob Hemmert of the Seminole County Sheriff's Department, but she might have just been angry over the publicity.

There are several indications, according to timelines, that Carl "Charlie" Brandt may have committed crimes throughout Florida, and also in Germany and Holland during the times he visited those countries.

Donald Withers remembered that when Charlie was doing "the blimp stuff" in the Keys, he got to be known as a pretty good programmer. They would send him to different places around the country and to Europe to do and teach programming, and he would only be gone for a couple of weeks at a time.

How many, Charlie? Jim was dying to ask. It was the only part of his life his friend had never bragged about. And if Charlie had been alive, and he and Jim were on his boat fishing, and Charlie had had his German knife, would there have been one more?

"You know how you have to fillet a fish properly before you cook it?" Detective Pat Diaz, from the Miami-Dade Police Department, Homicide Bureau, now retired, said. "Michelle Jones was filleted."

Donald Withers had become good buddies with Charlie while fishing for shark, and Donald was very experienced, very good at filleting fish. For that reason, whenever Donald and his friends would catch fish he would tell them to just let him handle it, because the rest would screw it up. However, Donald said he noticed Charlie's filleting and was impressed by it. After that, Charlie became the only person Donald would allow to fillet the fish with him. "Charlie was very, very good with a knife," Donald said.

SATAN IN PARADISE

During the winter of 1988 and summer of 1989, the residents of the Florida Keys were gearing up, not for another hurricane, but for something like a witch-hunt. It seemed a deranged butcher had slain two women and a little girl in a period of eleven months.

"These are the first mutilation murders we've had on the Keys in as long as most of us can remember," said one sheriff's deputy. "But we don't know if we've got a Satanic group, or just one lone nut."

The stories had been circulating along the ten-mile radius of Big Pine Key. First there was the brutal murder of four-year-old Patty Lorenza. She had been brought to a booze-filled, drug-riddled party that was dubbed by the local police as a "who's who of dirtbags."

After she was reported missing, investigators found her crime-scene in two parts. First, the child's panties and jumpsuit were found left as rape remnants in a patch of earth. Then they discovered the physical body, head smashed in, an image to be forever embedded in the detectives' minds. Brutalized with a blunt object and left as a free meal for another predator, she was relegated to the pages of a book chronicling the savagery of yet another monster. Six months had gone by and the stirring image of the Patty Lorenza murder hadn't rung any familiar bells in the minds of the locals. It was looked at as nothing more than an isolated, awful incident—until the evening of December 17, 1988.

A Michigan native, Lisa Sanders was a twenty-year-old petite woman who had challenged leukemia in a head-on battle and walked away alive, if not unscathed. Condemned to bone-weakening osteoporosis, she had decided to move into a little guesthouse of sorts behind her parents' home. It was there that the neighbors directly behind her had extended her an invite to a party. Sheltered and sickly as she was, a chance to mingle with the average crowd was to lonely Lisa like being asked out to the prom she'd missed. The party was being thrown on No Name Key, a place not noticeable to the passerby but well frequented by the high-school-to- college party crowd. Most of it is a wildlife refuge, houses are few and far between, and the only action travels up and down a two-way road, as Keys teenagers speed up to the spot where they spend their Friday nights. Along this rocky seacoast, Lisa Sanders would party till she came to the end of the road, and her life. After a falling-out with friends, Sanders decided to take the one-man path home. She never met her destination. Her mother became worried when Lisa did not meet her at a flea market the following day as planned, and she called the police. Deputies began to search but soon needed search no more. About a half-mile from the party where she went missing, vultures sounded the surrender of that scene, and Sanders's body was found. The young woman had been strangled, and smashed in the head with a blunt object, and her eyes had been gouged out by the brutal blade of a knife. Blood was everywhere up to about a quarter-mile away, in a field behind a rusted-out abandoned Volkswagen. Most of her heart and several vital organs were missing. The invasion of her flesh was so savage that even autopsy reports could not determine whether the body had been mutilated by a killer, or by the birds feasting on her freshly killed corpse.

The fate of thirty-nine-year-old Sherry Perisho was more certain in terms of the manner of death.

Her years alive were more left to chance. It was not whether she knew, but more so when she knew, to let the dice roll where it fell.

With her gorgeous looks and valedictorian grades, she had conquered the high-school arena and kicked dirt in the face of convention, choosing to follow the fork in the road leading to personal freedom. The shackles of her old life would no longer impede her, and if palm trees and sweaty skies would give her a chance at isolation, and a new start among the unjudged, then that is where she would aim body and mind at the speed of soul. This former beauty queen was looking for anything to shed her past image and catapult her into the spiritual self she felt burning at her inner core.

Sherry Perisho spent years writing her autobiography, which she titled, "An Act of God." She never got to finish it. She moved to Big Pine Key from New York, where she had relocated from Indiana. One of her entries read, "Spiritually, I didn't want to be dead at 21 like most country wives." Now she was thirty-nine, and no longer alive, but murdered.

"Julie…Julie, wake up… I think something awful has happened to Sherry." Just hours earlier, Clarence and Julie Shelmire had been out on the water under the Big Pine Key Bridge embracing the sweltering heat of July on a Wednesday afternoon, toying around on their jet skis as they occasionally did. At this point, they did not know a passing moment would turn into a permanent fixture in their minds. The sun was beginning to settle into dusk and what little light was left illuminated the small section of water containing the home of a resident with whom the couple was familiar: Sherry Perisho. It was 8:30 p.m. when Clarence and Julie had approached Perisho and the dinghy she called home. Perisho never used paddles, and would wade her small boat to and from shore. On this evening, the ten-footer had careened itself one hundred and fifty feet from the shoreline. Sherry had on a lightly colored sundress and welcomed the couple's friendly greeting. There was a brief bit of conversation and the Shelmires left feeling even better about their day because of Sherry's upbeat, positive mood—yet at the same time all three of them had been unknowingly in the crosshairs of Charlie Brandt.

"What, what is it?"

"I have this awful feeling something has happened to Sherry."

It wasn't a nightmare and it wasn't something physical. What had awoken Clarence was the sick feeling in his stomach and the racing of his heart; yet those were just symptoms of something larger, something everyone feels at one time or another in this life, yet can't quite pinpoint. For Clarence, the answer to his gut feeling would be provided just hours into the oncoming day; but for now, he was left with nothing more than the startling subconscious scream, and sheets soaked in sweat.

The night of July 19 was an uncomfortably hot night, and sweaty at ninety-five degrees. Roy and Nedra Plant had planned to spend the evening with their friends Dale and Rosemary Evans. The group of friends had gone about this routine numerous times before, and as night fell, they all made their way down to the north end of the North Pine Channel Bridge for an evening of fishing at the swimming hole. The full moon cast a welcoming spotlight on the area. They cast the first rod into the water at 9:00 p.m. After an hour and fifteen minutes of no luck, Roy cast out Nedra's pole, only to catch something that none of them could ever have prepared for. What first looked like a mannequin with a fishing hook in its left elbow would soon be identified as the cold, lifeless, disemboweled body of Sherry Perisho, floating face-down like a buoy left by the butcher.

In a fearful frenzy, Roy rushed to the local Tom Thumb store and alerted the police of this terrifying find. It wasn't long before yellow crime-scene tape lined the area like a grid, or a shark net.

As police canvassed the area, it wasn't too far down the embankment that they saw Sherry Perisho's most prized possession since she had retreated to the Keys: her dinghy, all ten feet of it, capsized in the water as if it were a symbol of how the life switch of her time on earth had been flipped as well. An underwater search uncovered Perisho's men's one-speed bike and bike basket containing a copy of the *New York Times*, Arrow trash bags, six packs of Bugler Tobacco, tan shorts, a bag with a used tampon, pink sunglasses, a Clorox bleach container, earphones to a radio, an Eveready flashlight, Skin So Soft lotion, insect repellent and a pack of Winston cigarettes. Also found were a blue-and-white umbrella, an orange life jacket, two gallon water jugs, a Coca-Cola can, a Grand Prize AM/FM pocket radio, a caramel corn container, and a red hip purse containing various batteries, a knife, lighters, pens, and cold-sore medicine.

The final two items were a Mickey Mouse blanket and a one-dollar bill which only brings to mind the meagerness for which her life was snuffed out, although that was clearly not the motive. This sad scene strewn with trivial items was all that was left to signal the last remnants of Sherry Perisho's tumultuous and sad, yet equally and beautifully inspiring path that she carved without fear or hesitation.

When the investigators responded, they found pentagrams in the area. "It appeared teenage kids had been doing that," said Sergeant Dennis Haley. When they retrieved her, they found her organs were removed, and her throat cut so many times her head was almost severed.

"She was eviscerated," Sergeant Patricia Dally stated.

There were both fingerprints found on the gunnel of the boat and palm prints found on the bottom of the boat. Neither belonged to Sherry Perisho. There was no DNA analysis back then, but there was a fingerprint database. Arresting officers must have taken Charlie Brandt's prints after he'd murdered his mother. And after Sherry Perisho's murder, investigators would have been able to run the prints found on her boat through the database. However, they had nobody to match them to.

If Charlie's prints had been on record, and not expunged because of his youth, he would have been nailed, and no more murders would have occurred—including Darlene Toler, Teri Helfrich Brandt, and Michelle Jones.

The newspapers, however, picked up on every rumor, and of course the tabloids dripped with Halloween scare headlines. The week before Halloween, on October 19, 1989, the *Weekly World News* announced, as though it were a concert, "SATAN IN PARADISE." The story's lead read: "A veil of terror has darkened a 10-mile stretch of the Florida Keys where two beautiful young women were fiendishly butchered by one or more Satanic cultists who ripped their hearts out."

The reporter managed to find one pious, well-meaning woman to corroborate his findings, a church worker who had counseled several cult members. "They're bored kids," she said. "They look very normal on the outside. They've been involved in initiations…used girls for ritual offerings on altars."

The fever surrounding the case, with its slew of suspects, never felt like it was going to break. On July 21, two days after the Perisho murder, the first suspect was interviewed. His name was Gary Paul Guekel. Guekel was originally confronted by an officer as he was crossing the street to go to the Summerland Key Quick-Mart. When the officer asked for his identification, Guekel explained that he had none, and that he was a wanted man in Washington State for auto-theft charges. When the officer patted him down, he didn't find anything suspicious and upon inspecting his bag, found only a pornographic magazine. The officer's eyes caught a possible red flag in the form of a scratched left cheek and busted lip. Were these wounds the work of a frantic Sherry Perisho, fighting for her life? The officer decided to take the man in for further questioning at the Big Pine Key substation. There the man explained that he did sleep under the Summerland Key Bridge, and that on the day of the murder he had been at the day labor hall and then had spent the evening hours drinking with his friends outside the Quick Mart. It was there that he fell into some work, when he met a father-son duo who hired him on to work construction the following day. As for the busted lip and scratched cheek? It was the result of a fight he had drunkenly gotten himself into and lost later that evening, when he'd returned to the bridge to crash out for the night. The officer found no evidence to link the man to the crime, and Washington State decided not to extradite him on his auto-theft charges. They let him go.

Five days later and Mike Felix Balogna was taken by Lieutenant Richard Conrady to the main headquarters of the Big Pine Key Sheriffs Office. Balogna was an interesting character who had spent the last few months of Sherry Perisho's snuffed-out life living with her on occasion. The dinghy she seemed so happy to call home, was provided to her by Balogna, and during those final months, the duo had maintained a sexual relationship. People who were questioned stated that Balogna was by far the closest person to Sherry during the days that served as a sad countdown toward her destruction. Balogna proclaimed his innocence in the crime and asked for a polygraph. After the test, Polygraph Examiner and Deputy Sheriff Mike Scott confirmed he was telling the truth. Balogna was cleared. An ex-roommate of Balogna's named Jim Sturgeon was also later contacted and polygraphed, but he too was cleared.

Twenty-six days later, on August 16, 1989, the phone line lit up at a Big Pine Key radio station. When the host picked up the phone, the voice on the other end stated that the killer of the girls (Patty Lorenza, Lisa Sanders, and Sherry Perisho) on Big Pine Key was a Mr. Robert Erwig. Fifteen minutes later, the ringing of a phone grabbed the attention of Detective Ed Miller, of the Monroe County Sheriff's Department. On the other end were the Metro–Dade crime stoppers and Officer Mike Cardenas informing Miller of a tip they had received that also pointed to Mr. Erwig as the perpetrator of the recent murders. The informant was an old neighbor of Erwig's who was constantly at odds with the man. His reasoning behind believing Erwig to be the killer was that the caller and Erwig had been in a heated argument, and Erwig had told the man if he complained to the police about him anymore, he would rip out the neighbor's heart. The neighbor, in what he described as fear for his life, fled the Keys. He told the officer that Erwig still lived in the last house on Mahogany Lane in Big Pine Key, that he was in his thirties and of German/Latin descent, with black hair and brown eyes and was known to work as a surgical assistant back in Pennsylvania.

Slightly over a month after Guekel was cut loose from the substation ,a man by the name of David Enulott, a local Radio Shack employee, had called police to inform them that he had recognized a photo of Sherry Perisho in one of the local newspapers, the *Key West Citizen*. He explained to the officer that Sherry Perisho had been a friend of his friend, a man named Hampton Kelly who would be filling in the slot for suspect number three. Hampton Kelley was a pleasant man when interviewed, one completely devoid of any knowledge of current news. His television didn't carry the local channels, nor did he read any local newspapers. When the officer showed him a picture of Sherry Perisho, he explained that he knew her but it had been at least a year prior when he'd last seen her. They met when she was hitchhiking along Stalk Island, a place where Sherry also had many friends. Hampton had picked her up, and she'd stayed with him. After several days she had left and for a while after that would stop by from time to time to stay for a few days. As time went on, Sherry Perisho ceased her visits and became an old memory in the mind of Mr. Kelly. He was cleared of any connection to the murder, but said he would show the photo around Stock Island to Sherry's friends in case they might be able to help.

Another month would go by and then, on October 12, 1989, Detective Ed Miller of the Monroe County Sheriff's Department received some photos from Detective Bob Schott of the Bartow Police Department. Schott explained how he had received some startling news during a telephone conversation. On the other end had been an FBI agent giving his take on the Perisho case, tipping Schott about the newest suspect. The man's name was Paul Crews, a white male, who was wanted in Bartow, Florida, for the brutal murder of a young white female named Clemmie Jewel Arnold, who was found in a remote area with her head barely hanging from her neck. The investigators on that crime believed the knife was too dull to fully sever the head. At that point the man had last been seen traveling through South Florida and South Carolina, where the woman's car was found. Crews was later found on the Appalachian Trail in Pennsylvania, after brutally murdering a young couple. In 1991, a Pennsylvania jury found him guilty of the murders in the trails, and Florida decided not to extradite him on the Clemmie Jewel Arnold case.

Former Monroe County Sheriff Rick Roth had a plausible hypothesis for the way in which Charlie might have approached Sherry Perisho and killed her without her seeing him, as was his usual M.O. She'd tied her boat close to shore, off a canal that cuts into Big Pine Key. "She was anchored on shore. She would go ashore to cook, and here was a canal that opened up into the bay right there, a canal that cuts into Big Pine Key. Sometimes she would cook in a little campground on shore."

As for the popular picnicking place for locals that Charlie and Teri frequented, Roth comes to the conclusion: "I wouldn't be surprised if he had met her before. The swimming hole was a mile from where she was found. I think he approached her on shore. I think the murder occurred on shore, but that is only my supposition. Either he threw her in the water or she was killed in the water."

It is a haunting image in any case—free-spirited Sherry Perisho cooking meat, her face lit from the front by the fires of the flames, and a shadowy figure approaching her from behind, intent on stealing her heart.

In 1989, right after Sherry Perisho was found murdered and mutilated, investigators brought in a profiler from the FBI.

It was at this time on October 22, 1989, that members of the FDLE and the FBI would combine their efforts to come up with a profile of the killer.

What can be made out of the profile is this:

The perpetrator probably does not own a vehicle, and if he drives one it would be a loaner belonging to a friend or a vehicle belonging to family or a mother or father. He would probably be incapable of maintaining a vehicle. This perpetrator is probably psychotic and is not polygraphable, as the perpetrator probably does not feel he has done something wrong or com-

mitted a criminal act. It is also highly probable that the perpetrator carries a pocketknife with him at all times. It is believed by the profilers that this individual will commit this type of crime again if he is not apprehended.

The perpetrator probably was a high-school graduate who is a loner and is considered to be a social outcast. He probably lives alone and is incapable of holding a regular job, and may work for one or two days at a time.

It is the profilers' belief that this perpetrator is not sexually active, and that the motive of the homicide was to remove the victim's heart. It is further believed by the profilers that the perpetrator intended to take the victim's head as well as the heart, due to the amount of damage done to the victim's neck. The profilers do not believe that the perpetrator of this homicide is not capable of raising children.

The profile was only spot-on about two things: The perp would pass a polygraph with flying colors. Not only did he feel absolutely no remorse for his crime, but actually relished it. If he took the body parts, he relived the crime and reveled in it. And, of course, the perpetrator would have no children. That was a decision he and his wife had already made.

The rest of the profile placed Charlie Brandt way off the radar.

On September 9, 1989, Stephanie Sheerer, who lives on a sailboat on Newfound Harbor—the same harbor where Sherry Perisho was found murdered and mutilated—explained to police that a man she knew by the name of Mike Dentini was someone who might be as a suspect. Stephanie Sheerer went on to explain that Dentini had been hanging out with Sherry Perisho frequently, as close to the day of the murder as the previous Friday. Unfortunately, it was not a friendly get-together. Sheerer stated that when she saw the two together down by the harbor, they were carrying on an argument that would leave Sherry clutching her cigarettes and pacing back and forth. Sheerer also stated that she had overheard a local couple heavily arguing not too long after the murder of Sherry Perisho. During this dispute, Sheerer claimed to have heard the woman yell, "Are you gonna kill me too, killer? Like you killed the little girl?" Later the woman was interviewed, and denied ever making that accusation. She and the man were eventually cleared of any involvement in the Perisho case.

Pamela Jean Evans, a Big Pine Key citizen for seven years, came to the police around this same time. She wanted to report strange phone calls she had received, in case the content of the calls could help police in any way, and also because the calls had begun to terrify her. When a woman was brutally beaten and raped on Big Pine Key earlier in the year, she had received a phone call from a man making obscene comments. Again, after Lisa Sanders was murdered, she'd received yet another antagonizing, threatening phone call. On July 17, just hours after Sherry Perisho had been disemboweled, Pamela received another perverse phone call. The last call had been on November 12, 1989. Was this the killer, stalking another woman? The answer, in time, would be no, but the fear in the community was already at an all-time high, and it was a fear that was gripping all of the female residents of the Florida Keys.

A local probation officer had phoned the police from her office explaining that on the night of Sherry Perisho's murder she'd witnessed a white Cadillac, driven by a white male, turn into the swimming hole at 6:40 p.m. This turned out to be another empty lead. Frustration mounted.

One Michael Eichmann was also brought in for questioning. He voluntarily gave a statement that he'd never had any sort of close relationship with Perisho and that, although the two of them had frequented the same swimming hole and area in general, her boat had never been anchored anywhere near his.

Another person questioned was Robert G. Rawls, who coasted the waters in his sailboat *Shangri-la*. Rawls was known to engage in satanic activity in the area and his boat had been anchored on or near No Name Key around the time of Lisa Sanders's murder. This was not known by investigators at the time of the interrogation.

Otis Nichols, a Big Pine Key citizen, was known to frequent the swimming hole to practice his martial arts. Three to four months prior to Sherry Perisho's death, he had been arrested for reckless display of weapons on Big Pine Key. He was known to have a mental problem.

Sean Carnes, another Big Pine Key resident, had informed police that two men, both poorly dressed and with bad teeth, and one of whom lived in the bushes, had made the statement that "This would be an easy one to take the heart out of."

Detectives Miller, Price, Robichaud, and Young canvassed the neighborhood conducting interviews and questioning locals as to whether or not they had seen anything or knew anything about the victim. The end of West Cahill Street overlooks the area where the murder had happened. The second house on that street was occupied by Kevin Wilhortte, who informed officers he knew the victim back when they had both lived at the Castaways Trailer Park, two or three months earlier. Wilhortte had no additional information as far as a personal connection, but informed officers of a suspicious van that had been hanging out by the swimming hole. He explained that the man who drove the yellow van was tall and skinny with a beard, and that he carried a goat in the back of the van. Wilhortte suspected the driver was involved in satanic activity in the area. Upon later investigation this van was ruled out as having anything to do with the case.

James and Roberta Spitzer had lived in Big Pine Key for three years and described a moderately heavyset man they had seen walking to and from the swimming hole, acting suspicious enough to stick in their memory. On the night of the murder, James claimed that he was driving over the bridge at 8:00 p.m. and briefly looked over, seeing Sherry Perisho's boat sunk with her umbrella submerged at the dinghy's side.

Billy Joe Shepherd was short, with graying hair, numerous tattoos, and a ninth-grade education. He had turned his vehicle, a light-blue 1968 Chevy pickup truck, into a makeshift home, and had turned a boat ramp at the west end of West Summerland Key into his property. The police were told to be on the lookout for the vehicle, based upon a witness mentioning it being in the background of a photo of Sherry Perisho in her dinghy taken just hours before her demise. When they came across it parked where its owner slept, the police noticed very suspicious items inside the vehicle. There were four knives, and on the dashboard of the trunk were two folding knives and one additional knife in a case. On the floor, peering out from underneath the passenger's side, was another knife. Also on the passenger's side, sticking out of a brown paper bag like some sort of perverse ornament, was a giant rubber dildo, coupled with a pornographic book in plain view. When Shepherd approached the vehicle, the police asked him to come to the substation, where they read him his rights, then performed a search on the vehicle to test for blood or any other evidence. While under interrogation, Shepherd said that Ed Banner, owner of the local B&B Auto Salvage Garage, had found a knife and given it to his son. When questioned about this, Banner explained he had found a knife and gave it to his son, but that was months before the murder. When police asked Banner what he knew about Shepherd, he offered a very interesting piece of information. Shepherd had told Banner that he was involved in cult activity and that people up in Ohio were trying to get him to do sinful things while simultaneously sending their people to follow him wherever he went. The last thing he had said to Banner was, "I wrestled with the Devil, and the Devil won."

Obviously there was no lack of leads in the murder of Sherry Perisho, but the case was growing cold. As investigators and other police officials know, crimes are not solved over a one-hour television slot, or even in a three-hour movie. And there was no shortage of Keys residents who knew, or were at least acquainted with, Sherry—but none who witnessed her murder.

The fever finally did subside, and the case was relegated to the cold-case files. Fifteen years would pass until the vision of the man hanging from his neck from the rafters in the garage of a young woman's house would heat it up again like a furnace.

What no one knew at the time of her murder was the real Sherry Perisho.

Sherry Perisho was supposedly a homeless transient who was a fixture in the area of Big Pine Key, which she had made her home when she first visited from New York, where she had previously moved from Illinois. She was nothing of the sort. To the locals, she was just Sherry. She was pleasant, and well-liked.

To understand some of this, it's important to understand the culture of the Florida Keys.

The motto of the Florida Keys is, "We seceded where others failed." The reason for the so-called secession, according to "conchs," or denizens of the Keys, was a decision by the U.S. Border Patrol to cut off the Keys from the mainland in the early 1980s, and to stop every car leaving the Keys, looking for illegal immigrants.

This, of course, caused not only an insurmountable traffic jam, but paralyzed tourism, the main income of the islands. So in 1982, the mayor of Key West, Dennis Wardlow, along with a handful of powerful community leaders, decided to secede. They raised their own flag, along with the U.S. flag, and even issued a secession proclamation.

The locals felt justified in keeping to their freewheeling yet low-key and non-judgmental lifestyle, and everyone was welcome to paradise— except for when Satan paid a visit.

It is a beautiful, breezy, calm, friendly, "lazy-days" place. It is a place where people from all walks of life are accepted, and sometimes embraced.

Oftentimes one cannot tell the difference between a CEO or a street person by just looking at them. According, there is no or little judgment of people regarding their "status in life," or past. It is a small community where everyone knows one another, even though there are a large number of transients.

Sherry Perisho was known to many people in the Big Pine area. She was seen frequently at the local convenience store on Big Pine Key. Although she opted to live in her dinghy—despite the invitations of some friends to come and stay at their homes—she was a familiar presence to those who lived and worked in the area. She was known to engage in prostitution, but she was not judged or scorned. After all, she did this only when she needed money for food. Also, she had a circle of friends and boyfriends from time to time. She lived in her dinghy at the east end (or north end for non-Keys folk) of the Big Pine Channel Bridge. She would sit on top of or in her little boat on the shore, visible to all. She heard communicating with the planet Saturn and singing out loud. She was a beautiful woman, and the image fit—a strange mermaid floating on the waves, singing the song of the sirens.

This area was also known as the "swimming hole," where many locals would go to party and swim. It was not a secluded area; it could be seen from the main roadway. In fact, there was a picture of Charlie at a party at the swimming hole, which would not have been uncommon since he lived in the area. There are other photos of Charlie and Teri picnicking here. Coincidentally, or on purpose, Charlie has his back to the camera in those photos.

On the date of her murder, Sherry Perisho was last seen sitting on her boat on the shore, reading a newspaper. It was around 8:00 or 8:30 p.m. At that time of year it is still somewhat light out and she was visible. Charlie's house was across the highway, a couple of blocks in. He would have seen her presence in that area regularly. It was highly likely they crossed paths at the local store. He would have known she was there, and it is conceivable that he targeted her in advance because she was visible and available. After all, there she was, every day, in various stages of dress or undress—the watery temptress, Saturn's Secret.

In 1989, right after Sherry Perisho was found mutilated, investigators brought in a profiler from the FBI.

She said the killer was way off the radar and not at all like one of the residents, but also a street person or a transient. She added that he had never maintained a "healthy relationship," especially with women. The police department focused on bringing in every transient and homeless person in the Florida Keys, much as the Border Patrol had when the Conch Republic seceded.

At first, when the Sheriff's Department began their investigation and were canvassing the neighborhood door-to-door and stopping cars, they'd uncovered a witness, a woman who described a man running across the street. They didn't put much stock in that witness, even though they took her to Ft. Lauderdale to a sketch artist. But Sherry Perisho's murder investigation eventually went cold, with nobody to claim her and nobody to miss her except the ocean, who was her only friend. Perhaps if the neighborhood canvass had continued just a couple of houses down, Teri Brandt would have told investigators about the fish-cleaning room.

FREEDOM'S JUST ANOTHER WORD
FOR NOTHING LEFT TO LOSE...

And so long as you haven't experienced
This: to die and so to grow,
You are only a troubled guest
Of the dark earth

      — Goethe, "The Holy Longing"

But somebody cared about Sherry Perisho—somebody missed her terribly, and claimed her by writing letter after letter to the Monroe County Sheriff's Office for anything that might tell her why Sherry had moved to Big Pine Key, and why she had been murdered.

Her first cousin, Marilyn Angel, was also her best friend, and her surname fits. She wanted to protect Sherry's reputation, and was incensed when her cousin was called a prostitute. She even wrote a letter to a television station in Miami when they showed her cousin's body, nude, floating in the water. "If you show one, you have to show them all!" she wrote.

Investigators found stuck inside her dinghy, among the deceased woman's things, an autobiography Sherry Perisho was writing. It is, of course, incomplete. The last chapter was written in blood by Charlie Brandt.

What the autobiography—which Sherry was in the process of getting copyrighted—reveals, is an infinitely more complex portrait than that of "the homeless transient" who is mentioned in passing by all the media covering the case. She was more like "The Outsider," from the book of the same title by Colin Wilson—a landmark investigation into alienation in literature and in life.

She was born in Terre Haute, Indiana, and she and her mother lived in a series of trailer parks. Then they moved to Illinois, where Sherry started high school. Something she wrote at the time summarizes her restlessness and curiosity about the world: "Spiritually, I didn't want to be dead at 21 like most country wives."

She recounted how her father taught her to swim at the age of three by simply throwing her in the ocean, while "Mother taught me to make paper flowers colored with lipstick to sell in the bars for a dollar. Dad would give me a little sip of beer in a glass and encourage me to pan handle change from the men he worked with." Sherry Perisho was well prepared, from earliest infancy, for life on the road—or in the ocean, as evidenced by another entry:

"We visited Cypress Gardens. Sometimes Dad would rent a cabin cruiser and take us deep-sea fishing. The dock was busy and clean. The north had left me sad."

According to her autobiography, Sherry felt a "sadness," or "depression," or worse yet, "alienation," whenever she was in colder climates. In other words, apparently, whenever she was not in Florida.

"I missed the sun and the beach," she writes. Happily the wandering family settled in the Sunshine State.

According to the writer, she was, and was reputably acknowledged as being, "psychic." Whether there is such an explanation for this, and whether it be coincidence, precognition, or just a bad dream, is still an enigma.

"Although really not a mind reader, I wanted to know about sex and crime. I had scored 85% on tests given by psychics at Duke University and occasionally had uncanny dreams. Later, while studying death and violence, I realized that violent and primitive scenes may have laid the foundation for one of the more shocking and violent of all my occult experiences. At the age of four, I slept in the upstairs…room of a large house in St. Petersburg. We were several miles from the beach with senior citizens. I had begun to withdraw; my hair had turned blonde from sleeping tightly curled on one end of the bed like a rabbit. I'll describe the nightmare. About dusk or twilight I saw my father seated in a wheelchair in front of a motel near a heavily wooded area. Three men stood behind him. I noticed the middle-man suddenly raise a chainsaw and slice the top of my father's head off.

After the nightmare, my father found work in Washington and asked my aunt and uncle to put me on a plane. I remember the trip very distinctly."

A dream of decapitation is certainly a coincidence, though some may think that it is not. After Sherry Perisho's murder, the Medical Examiner found her head almost severed from her body. Her heart was never found.

When she was a young girl, she also had a Howdy Doody marionette; it took hours to untangle the strings. And the children laughed at "Charlie the Bartender," whose face would light up and smoke would pour out of his ears whenever he took a drink. That is obviously a coincidence as well, but is, in retrospect, grotesquely poetic, like a Grimm's fairy tale.

And then the "alienation" seeps in, as well as Sherry Perisho's precociousness and the angst that went with it.

"I started exhibiting some coldness and alienation. I became instantly aware of time and a silent inner and outer dimension. At seven, I was acutely conscious of the microscopic and atomic worlds."

According to her, her I.Q. tested out at 136 in primary school, which indicates a superior intelligence. "As I studied drawing, poetry, and music I was sorely piqued over my lack of imagination and considered it also a handicap." This "lack of imagination" may have played a part in her choice of action, or inaction, much later on, when she moved to Big Pine Key and opted to live in a dinghy under the bridge.

What is known, again, from her writings, is that the young woman did despise whatever she considered "bourgeois" or conformist.

"My aunt and uncle's home was quite comfortable, furnished in expensive maple and carpeted. They wore expensive clothing and enjoyed television. Although they loved art, they would never give up the comforts of home to run away. Artists and radicals were frightening, although they were of the same fibre as the original prairie settlers."

She might not have become "an original prairie settler," but chose the ocean for other reasons.

Another entry:

"Not only was depression a constant presence in my life, it was the keystone to an event that became a turning point in my life.

"As I stood in the honeysuckle-covered back porch, I was struck by the hideous ugliness of my environment. In five seconds, the sky had darkened and ping-pong-size balls of hail began to rain from the firmament.

"I connected the terrible weather and depressed state I was casually familiar with American Indian rain dancers and The English version of dowsers and thought if it was possible I would set about to reverse the effect as an alternative heating source for northern climates."

Sherry Perisho was often observed gazing at the sky from her dinghy, and trying to communicate with the planets out loud. She loved astronomy from a very early age, she writes.

"Staying out at night to study the skies, I studied charts of the constellations and the Greek and Roman mythology about them.

"The mystery of the universe intrigued me. I fought my doubts about the power of the mind. Is it possible to read minds? Is the spoken language simply the pyrotechnics of pre-recorded genetic material?"

Later, as she matured, Sherry would test some of these theories by pushing her personal boundaries.

She mentions becoming a contestant in beauty pageants, and winning some of them. She doesn't seem to attach any importance to this, as if the events don't carry any sense of reality. Instead, she pens her thoughts about social injustice.

"News of the American farmer on the media seemed to consist of pictures of deplorable poverty and food stamps. The universe seemed to consist of haves and have-nots, and a have-not generally had 'have not' permanently stamped on his forehead. The general working class couldn't even understand the state or government policy, and had never even read a hardcover book on economics from end to end. Lay-offs meant unbearable cutbacks and violence."

As far as a personal romantic life, Sherry Perisho is equally casual and detached.

She met a young hockey player from Chicago at age thirteen, and although she had no knowledge of sex, he became the first boy to make love to her, and in half a minute.

And then, in her usual cavalier way, she writes, as if all in one breath and in one sentence.

"I managed to get elected as Freshman Class President and managed to get engaged before my sixteenth birthday. I was on decorating committees and spent a lot of time at the apple grower's house. His physique was unimpressive and he suffered from Huntington's chorea but his hair was blonde, his eyes were green and he was quite intelligent. Sometimes at night, we drove to the orchard and parked by the lake, to make love.

We talked about everything under the sun. From Mary Baker-Eddy, the founder of Christian Science, to Impressionist art. He made a good lover, strong and enduring. I reached sexual fulfillment and would have remained faithful till the end. We used birth control."

As emotionally disconnected as the romance started, it ended, and Sherry is not sorry.

"I was relieved. I had wanted to marry a more attractive man and gave his diamond back."

At this point, she seemed somewhat disconnected, and too concerned about national and world issues than her to care much about own microcosm.

"1965 had been the beginning of the bad times both for me and for the nation. The escalation of the Vietnam conflict made it a national issue. The evening news reports were full of bombings and massacres. Anti-war protesters began to flood the capital. Human rights activists like Martin Luther King began to appear making speeches for radical changes in society."

She was obviously either influenced by the feminist movement, or might have been a forerunner of it as she writes:

"As to sleeping with a man without benefit of clergy when younger, I felt if I wasn't pregnant there were no charges. The person and the time and place weren't unpleasant. A cosmopolitan person would survive countless extra-marital experiences and multiple marriages. The only bad experiences were due to exploitation and lack of choices."

Again, the incipient detachment seeps into her writing.

She had a "flirtatious affair with an older man." According to her writings, the man was married and poor. She got pregnant. She arranged for an abortion. The older man introduced her to his best friend.

This cannot really be interpreted as coldness—given the writer's intensity and longing for something more—let alone promiscuity. Sherry Perisho was more or less, in her own words, a student of life, with all the disconnect and detachment that entails. At this point, she might have been headed for a nervous breakdown, or a bout of enlightenment.

And then, in the depths of another depression, she called "the friend," and figured it "might be healthier to move to New York or California."

The man asked her to marry him over the phone. She blurted out an acceptance and they eloped in the summer.

It was a practical decision for her.

"Marrying him would mean better quarters and my choice of schools. I wouldn't be bothered with a haphazard courtship and ugly scenes.

"I think there are these reasons why women get married: Ideology, economics, and politics. I had married for ideological reasons."

These don't seem like hidden agendas, or taking advantage of someone, in Sherry Perisho's mind and heart. Everything was logical, everything out in the open. Everything was thought out so it might lead unin-terruptedly to her field of study. Except in this particular case, things did not go as she wished.

Again she narrates objectively, as if she weren't in the picture:

"Our first months together didn't turn out well. I was depressed and stayed home while looking for a job. Our sex life dribbled down to a forced performance. I was frigid and after a couple months gave up hav-ing sex at all. The Americans landed on the moon." She attaches the same important to her sex life as to hearing about the astronauts landing on the moon.

Sherry writes that she "took a drive to Ball State," the university, took the exam for advanced placement, and re-enrolled as a pre-med student. She started in December of 1970.

However, "Between school, 15-20 hours of part-time work, a husband and a seven-room home I was hustling."

And then she began to study Eastern philosophy, and about rein-carnation she ponders: "I felt reincarnation is only a feeling gotten from prerecorded genetic material filtering through the subconscious."

Then, more importantly:

"I felt that God and the Holy Spirit are a phenomena of conscious-ness and enlightenment. The Devil was the embodiment of the uncon-sciousness."

Consciousness and enlightenment and the embodiment of the un-consciousness. Sherry Perisho had only begun to tap what made her and Charlie Brandt polar opposites.

And then, once again, her marriage end. She writes about it in dis-parate yet connected sentences that evidence the same detachment as before.

"I was depressed and suicidal. I wanted a divorce. I masturbated. I hated Ken for not being a good sexual partner. I wished I had more mon-ey. I wanted to run away. I didn't know what sex and romance was if I had it. Watergate hit the news. I wanted a baby."

She took a new course offered by the university. "Death and Violence."

Almost prophetically, she later writes: "Spiritual death could occur as a strangulation, drowning or beheading. I had choked on society, drowned on emotionalism, and needed strong identification to survive crises."

There is no way, or is there, that Sherry Perisho would have known where her physical, or spiritual death, would occur, but it is possible that some people sense, preternaturally in some way, the manner in which they will leave this earth.

By this time, Sherry had separated from her then husband at the age of twenty-one, and she writes:

"Dr. Timothy Leary of California had made news with his experience in the use of mind-altering drugs. Several members of major rock groups had been arrested for possession of marihuana. Abbie Hoffman had been arrested in Chicago." Hoffman was a founder of the self-titled "Yippies," and accused of being an anti-government revolutionary.

A friend at Ball State University asks her if she wants to move to New York.

"Medical school could wait. I was free and unhandicapped by children or a spouse. New York could be fun."

She shares an apartment on the Upper East Side. She starts an interior decorating business. She makes money. She collects and studies art.

And then, from her rich artist friends who had a lot of very rich patrons, she began to experiment with psychedelic drugs. This could have led to the breakdown that eventually took her to Big Pine Key.

"I learned to drink champagne and smoked a little grass. Poppers, amyl nitrate, had us on the floor on our hands and knees giggling uncontrollably.

I did acid and Quaaludes, peyote and Digoxin, THC and cocaine.

I took speed and worked continuously for three days."

In her quest for self-knowledge and to know the universe around her,

Sherry studied parapsychology in New York, began to subscribe more to Eastern philosophies like Buddhism, and read Aldous Huxley's *The Doors of Perception*, in which Huxley chronicles his experience with psychedelic drugs. It was also the source of the name Jim Morrison took for his band, "The Doors."

As she studied and read, she writes, "evil began to creep into my life." Perisho never fully explains what this "evil" is, but she does qualify it by writing: "It was difficult to maintain what Easterners refer to as the cloud state."

This is when she began to experiment with extra-sensory perception and out-of-body experiences by delving "into Body in Pain and the imagination. From 1977 to the present I virtually lived on the street, experiencing starvation, over-exertion and exposure to the elements. Over-exertion seemed to be the primary key to any extra-sensory powers concerning the climate."

Sherry read Carlos Castaneda, who wrote about extra-sensory perception from psychedelic experiences, Native American "guides," and his reclusive, mind-opening trips with peyote into the primeval jungles.

She concludes: "I managed to come through the vulgar experience of becoming aware, both from drug and non-drug-related experiences."

"Vulgar?" Did she long for more?

"From Eastern books describing the anima and animus I sorted through voices and sensations, choosing the path to spiritual freedom."

Freedom is what she sought to attain, why she went through such extremes of mind and body. "Freedom's just another word for nothing left to lose," Janis Joplin had sung.

Then Sherry read the most romantic "outsider," as Colin Wilson, the English writer, dubbed the German novelist Herman Hesse.

"I read Herman Hesse, titles like 'Siddhartha,' 'Steppenwolf' and 'Damian,' books describing man's struggle with the soul in crisis. Since moving to New York my sleep had become the background for several occult experiences."

And then, some experiences occur:

"While practicing meditation and mindfulness at a yoga club upstate I had several visionary experiences. One rather pleasant one occurred in the afternoon. I had fallen asleep and woke up with the sensation I was floating several feet above the ground. The roof to the little cabin had disappeared and my instructor had appeared at the door and spoke to me.

"I had witnessed a "floating" after-death experience once while lying in bed in my apartment in New York. I awoke from sleep one evening to find a 'man' or 'warlock' attempting to strangle me. Telling myself I was still dreaming and had 'summoned' the assassin. Although my experiences are due to what Indians called the 'third eye,' westerners know it as the subconscious and imagination. They happened so rarely I regarded them as a thanatopic experience and kept track of them as a register of good health. I feel the pre-recorded messages stored in the gene were a plausible source for all powers."

One wonders if she felt her real murder and dismemberment, inside her dinghy and lying on the bottom of the little boat, as one of those nightmares.

At this point, her regimen to overcome human wants and sensations became more rigorous and earnest. She was certainly headed downward at this point.

"I returned to New York in the fall of 1979, and continued an exercise program combined with dance. I managed to earn a few dollars with this method. In my resting hours I meditated and tried to transcend lesser wants and feelings. Much had happened to me. Short of amputation I had felt more intensive pain than could be endured by the human mind or body. No one and nothing existed. I was no longer cold, no longer hungry, the outside world no longer mattered…as spring came I took occasional walks, but the spontaneous ability to react had been erased from life.

"The world was full of a stillness. If it just remained the same, that seemed satisfaction enough. I had no more energy to fight any more 'devils.'"

Did Sherry fight Charlie Brandt under the Big Pine Key Bridge in

1989? Had her "ability to react" been "erased from life?" Was she unable, or unwilling, to fight the Devil himself?

But at this point she met another man, another "outsider" to accompany her in her travels to the outer limits.

"Ken Hall was a tall platinum blonde of Swedish descent. His ice-blue eyes looked over an aquiline nose and thin-lipped curved mouth. He played classical guitar and worked as a carpenter. We spent the summer out-of-doors, eating the food and smoking the cigarettes people gave to us. I smoked a little now and then, a leftover from a lack of stimulants. As we trailed through New York, we set destinations at least a hundred blocks away; such as, Let's walk to Harlem, or Let's do all of Central Park today. We carefully pushed our bodies to the limit.

"Social Security had granted a check for $2300 and a small monthly check of $370."

Still, like most outsiders, she was not happy, although she had some small resources to live on. "I was alone, a hapless scientist, with no equipment, no computer, no expert to explain the details...I was steeled for a future world of space travel and super powers likened only to Star Trek: "world of interplanetary travel at the wink of an eye."

Sherry Perisho's very last entry in her autobiography reads: "As I am writing, I have nearly succeeded and hope to next attend law school."

Law school was not to be, as Sherry, for some reasons unbeknownst to anyone, then moved from New York to Big Pine Key.

In retrospect, it now seems inevitable that Charlie Brandt and Sherry Perisho would meet at that fatal juncture called "the swimming hole" under the Big Pine Key Bridge. They almost seem like characters out of the analysis of the outsider in literature, from Colin Wilson's book.

Charlie Brandt: "An Existentialist monster who rejects all thought, a Mitya Karamazov without an Ivan or an Alyosha to counterbalance him. He reaches beyond prohibitions, beyond natural instinct, beyond morality...(he) loves nothing and everything. He is primeval matter, monstrous soul form..."

Mitya Karamazov is Dimitri Karamazov in the Dostoievsky novel, *The Brothers Karamazov*. Mitya is primitive and hedonistic; Ivan is his intellectual brother, and Alyosha his saintly one. Charlie Brandt did not have the two latter aspects incorporated into his alter ego.

Sherry Perisho, on the other hand, is akin to the heroine of Henry James's <u>Portrait of a Lady</u>, Isabel Archer:

"Her social success in English society leads a very eligible English Lord to propose to her; she refuses him because she feels that life is far too full of exciting possibilities to narrow it down so soon…She too is 'defeated by life,' by her own inability to live at a constant intensity."

When referring to German author Herman Hesse, whom Sherry read, Wilson states:

"He has a deep sense of the injustice of human beings having to live on such a lukewarm level of everyday triviality; he feels there should be a way of living with the intensity of the artist's creative ecstasy all the time."

Both Charlie Brandt and Sherry Perisho sought freedom in different ways: Charlie, by living in the present, his "glazed look" transporting him into the inner world of joy where he could satisfy his primitive instincts; Sherry, by pushing herself to the limits and surviving in the simplest way she knew how, while always reaching for the stars, or the artist's ecstasy.

Each of them hailed from different towns in Indiana: Sherry from Terre Haute, and Charlie from Fort Wayne. Both moved to Big Pine Key, and there, under the Big Pine Key Bridge, and in the dinghy that had brought Sherry so much freedom, they were fated to collide.

Charlie Brandt was, in a word, an Existentialist interloper.

And Sherry Perisho, in her own way, summoned up the Devil himself.

This is the autopsy report from Sherry Perisho's murder, now a case number at the Monroe County Sheriff's Department, where she was liked by all law-enforcement officers, as well as by the residents of Big Pine Key. In 2008, the department built a memorial in honor of all Brandt's victims, and placed flowers around Sherry Perisho's dinghy that had been her home:

OFFICE OF THE MEDICAL EXAMINER
DISTRICT SIXTEEN—MONROE COUNTY
FISHERMEN'S HOSPITAL* MARATHON, FLORIDA 33050
PERISHO, Sherry
ME89-128/K89-9842
DOD July 19, 1989
Found 22:20 hours

AUTOPSY REPORT

Deceased alleged to be Sherry Perisho. Autopsy begun at Fishermen's Hospital morgue in Marathon, Florida, on July 20, 1989, at 0:57 hours. Autopsy performed by R. J. Nelms, Jr., M.D., Medical Examiner. Identification of remains by Monroe County Sheriff's Office. Investigating officer assigned to the case is Detective Jerry Powell of Monroe County Sheriff's Office, Key West. Remains transported from the scene by Bill Sutton, Chief Forensic Investigator. Present at the examination are Bill Sutton, Ronald Hartman (paramedic), Detective Trish Almeda, Detective Lt. Conradi, and Deputy Greenwood.

EVIDENCE OF INJURY: The anterior neck is slashed open with a 27.0 cm incised wound and two additional incised wounds above the larger wound at each end of the larger wound measuring 9.0 cm in length on the right an 5.0 cm in length on the left. There is also a stab wound on the right upper anterior neck measuring 17.7 cm in width with the sharp end of the wound toward the right. The right carotid artery is severed with a clean cut and exposed, and white foam is noted in the trachea, which has also been severed with a clean cut as well as the underlying esophagus. There are two superficial stab wounds of the left neck and shoulders apparently angling toward the left as they enter, the one further left imbedding in shoulder bone, with the sharp edge pointing upward and measuring 2.1 cm in length. There are also cut marks on the anterior vertebral column of the neck. The chest and abdomen have been slashed open with a fairly continuous incised wound extending from the pubis up to the 1st rib with serrated marks in the mid portion of the wound, exposing bowel in the abdomen and the sternum. The right nipple has been cut off. In the addition, the sternum has been slashed open in the mid portion up to the 7th rib where the incision angles toward the left imbedding into the left 1st rib. There is an anterior laceration and opening of the pericardial sac, and the heart is absent with the aorta and pulmonary artery cut cleanly across and the right atrium mostly removed except for one small fragment. There is an estimated 1000 cc of blood present in the left pleural cavity, but none in the right pleural cavity. There is a large laceration through the diaphragm with a deep incised wound of the liver in the left lobe near the mid portion of the liver as well as smaller incised or stab wounds of the left lobe of the liver and one small stab wound of the right superior anterior mid lobe of the liver. There are multiple perforations of bowel and mesentery, small bowel. There are red colored bruises of the scalp, three in the occipital area and two in the frontal area measuring up to 3.0 cm with no underlying injury of the skull or brain.

There are two green bruises or contusions of the lower leg interiorly near the ankles and a superficial scratch of the left arm, purple contusion of the right upper arm measuring 6.0 cm, a blue contusion of the right posterior upper arm measuring 2.0 cm, and two green defensive contusions of the left forearm. There are scattered green contusions of the left lateral foot. The clothing is blood soaked, but the bikini pants and overriding white warm up pants do not have cuts. The upper bra strap has been cut, and the cup from one side of the bra is missing. There is also a cut into the upper anterior white shirt near the neck wounds. No blood is remaining in the blood vessels of the body. There is retroperitoneal hemorrhage of the right *lower abdomen in the region of the inferior vena cava.*

EXTERNAL EXAMINATION: *The body is that of an unembalmed well-developed well-nourished Caucasian female weighing approximately 130 pounds, measuring 62 inches, representing the stated age of 39 years, clad in blue bikini pants and blue bikini bra which is loose, white warm-up shirt and white warm-up pants, all wet and blood stained. There is a fishhook with ballyhoo bait hooked to the pants. In general, the skin is well tanned in a bikini distribution, body hair is normal in distribution, the hair of the legs is unshaven, the scalp is intact, and scalp hair is brown and medium long with a red beret. In general, the face is intact and uninjured. The pupils are 7.0 mm and equal and irises are blue. The ears are intact without earrings. The nose is intact, symmetrical, and both flares are patent. The mouth contains natural teeth, but the upper teeth are in poor repair, missing all upper incisors with two small caps, the right lower molar is missing. The right upper molar in the rear is capped, the left upper premolar is capped, and the left lower front molar has a yellow metal inlay. The mouth contains some foamy white to clear fluid. Lips are intact. The neck shows no fractures of dislocation of vertebral column. The chest is symmetrical and intact except for previously mentioned injuries. The back is clear with a few scattered acne scars. Axillae are clear. The abdomen has a lower mid vertical abdominal scar measuring 14.0 cm in length. The genitalia are normal adult female and the rectum is unremarkable grossly. No jewelry is noted. Buttocks, legs, and arms show normal development, and there is a 3.0 cm scar on the left dorsal foot. There is full rigor mortis of all muscle groups at 1:30 AM, but at the scene at approximately 10:30 to 11:00, no rigor mortis was noted. Minimal posterior purple lividity is present.*

INTERNAL EXAMINATION: *The viscera of the neck are present but disrupted. The thyroid gland is grossly normal and retracted upward with the trachea.*

On examination of the thoracic cavity, the pleural surfaces are smooth and glistening, and the right pleural space is free of excess fluid. The peri-cardial sac is smooth and glistening and but contains no fluid. The heart is absent (see Evidence of Injury). Major vessels are devoid of blood (see Evidence of Injury).

The larynx, trachea, bronchi are filled with foamy fluid. Lungs show min-imal anthracosis, but both are enlarged and heavy due to copious quantities of pulmonary edema, the right weighing 985 grams and the left 860 grams.

On examination of the abdominal cavity, the fatty panniculus measures 3.0 cm. The peritoneal surfaces are smooth and glistening, there is no excess fluid or adhesions, and abdominal organs are in proper position. The mu-cosa of the entire GI tract is generally intact except for occasional puncture wounds of the small bowel, and the appendix is present and uninjured. The stomach contains an estimated 150 cc of food and fluid consisting of toma-toes, watermelon seeds, peanuts, popcorn seeds, cottage cheese, and zucchini or pickle like green vegetable fragments. Small bowel and colonic contents appear normal. The liver weighs exactly 1470 grams and cut surface is normal without evidence of scarring. The gallbladder is normal and the biliary system is patent. The pancreas has normal contour, size, and position. Cut surface reveals the normal tan lobular appearance. The spleen weighs exactly 110 grams with slight wrinkling of the capsule. Its cut surface appears normal.

On examination of the retroperitoneal and pelvic structures, the ad-renal glands are normal in position and appearance. The kidneys have the usual bean-shaped contour and each weighs exactly 100 grams. The cortex measures 0.7 cm and the medulla 1.2 cm in thickness. Collecting systems are patent and normal. Urinary bladder is contracted and devoid of urine with normal mucosa. The uterus is normal in appearance. Fallopian tubes have been severed with the distal ends absent. The ovaries are normal in ap-pearance, and one contains a corpus luteum with central gray zone. Lymph nodes are small and visible but unremarkable.

On examination of the cranial cavity, the skull is intact. No internal bleeding is noted. The cranial fossae are intact and sella turcica appears normal. Pituitary gland is grossly normal. The brain weighs exactly 1350 grams. *The gyri and sulci are of normal width. Cranial blood vessels are patent without evidence of significant arteriosclerosis or congenital anomalies. Sectioning of the brain reveals no abnormalities.*

TOXICOLOGY EXAMINATION: Blood in NaF tubes and serum are collected. Blood is collected in EDTA tubes and turned over to Detective Trish Almeda of Monroe County Sheriff's Office. A "rape kit" is collected with oral, vaginal, and rectal swabs; fragments from skin; combed and plucked pubic hairs; and plucked scalp hairs; and all are turned over to the Sheriff's Department.

MICROSCOPIC EXAMINATION:

Cardiovascular: Sections of atrium reveal no abnormalities of endocardium, myocardium, or epicardium. Sections of pericardium reveal acute hemorrhage in the adventitial fat.

Respiratory: Sections of lung reveal areas of pulmonary edema and minimal anthracosis. Alveolar spaces and walls are fairly normal in appearance.

Gastrointestinal: Section of esophagus is unremarkable as is section of appendix. Small bowel is relatively well preserved with slight postmortem autolysis of surface mucosa. Section of colon reveals a small amount of recent hemorrhage in the submucosa. Section of stomach and small bowel at pylorus reveals fairly well preserved mucosa with only superficial early postmortem sloughing and no significant underlying pathology.

Liver and Gallbladder: Gallbladder is well preserved except for loss of mucosal cells, and there appears to be underlying chronic cholecystitis. Sections of liver are well preserved with normal architecture. No evidence of scarring or inflammation. Areas of congestion are evident to a mild degree, particularly subcapsular, and there is one area of recent hemorrhage in soft tissues adjacent to liver.

Pancreas: Well preserved with no signs of postmortem autolysis and no ab-normalities noted.

Spleen: A suggestion of focal subcapsular recent hemorrhages, otherwise no abnormalities.
Genitourinary: Sections of kidney are well preserved without evident ab-normalities. Urinary bladder wall is unremarkable. One section of ovary shows corpus albicantia and another shows active corpus luteum. Section of cervix shows mild chronic cervicitis with squamous metaplasia.

Endocrine: Pituitary gland is unremarkable. Thyroid and adrenal glands are likewise normal in appearance.
Lymphatic: Sections of three lymph nodes are unremarkable. One shows mild anthracosis and is therefore probably hilar in origin.

Infrequent germinal centers are present in a normal frequency.

Central Nervous System: Section of medulla oblongata is well preserved and unremarkable. Section of pans reveals no abnormalities. Sections of cerebellum, dentate nucleus, and hippocampus are likewise unremarkable. Sections of basal ganglia and cerebral cortex are generally unremarkable. One small focus of calcification is present in one section of cerebral cortex in the adjacent white matter.

ANATOMICAL DIAGNOSES:

1. Incised wound of chest with excision of heart and right nipple, left hemothorax, lacerations of pericardium, diaphragm, and liver.
2. Incised wound of abdomen with multiple punctures of small bowel and mesentery and right retroperitoneal hemorrhage.
3. Incised wounds of neck transection of right carotid artery, trachea,

and esophagus, and exsanguination.

  4. Severe pulmonary edema secondary to salt water drowning.

  5. Chronic cholecystitis.

  6. Chronic cervicitis with squamous metaplasia.

  7. Recent hemorrhage, colon, liver, spleen, pericardium.

  8. Focal calcification, cerebral white matter, significance undetermined.

CAUSE OF DEATH: Salt water drowning and exsanguination due to trau-matic wounds.

MANNER OF DEATH: Homicide.

TOXICOLOGY FINDINGS: Negative. See attached report.

R.O. Nelms, Jr., M.D.
Medical Examiner
District Sixteen
Monroe County, Florida
It states there were no drugs found in her system.

Marty Helfrich Morgenrath, Teri and Mary Lou's sister, remembered something peculiar about the Sherry Perisho case.

"The last time we were there, at Charlie and Teri's home on Big Pine Key, my husband and I wanted to go kayaking. I looked at renting [a kayak], and then we both decided to buy one and keep it there at their house. So we went kayaking several times, and Teri got very upset about that, and we found that strange, because we only went to visit once every two or three years. Then, later, when we went back, we'd realized we kay-aked right past where Sherry Perisho's boat was."

Nobody knows whether Teri Helfrich Brandt knew with any degree of certainty whether her husband Charlie was responsible for the murder of Sherry Perisho. But everyone was certain that if she subconsciously knew, she was in deep denial about it, and it cost her her life.

In 2004, Seminole County investigators conducted an interview with Patricia McClintock, or Pat Helfrich, the second-oldest of Teri's sisters after Mary Lou, Michelle's mother.

Pat had spent a lot of time with her baby sister and her new brother-in-law, and found them to be madly in love with each other. Charlie did not want children, and the sister thought Charlie felt they would take all the attention away from him, "since [he and Teri] were so into each other." But then, Pat also recalled that Charlie never talked about his family. And then came the "glazed look" that everyone talked about. "There were sometimes you couldn't talk to Charlie," the sister explained. "It was like he wasn't there."

"They both drank quite a bit," she said. "I would say my sister was a borderline alcoholic. And when she drank, she could really push buttons."

Pat experienced this during an excursion to Europe with her youngest sister. "I took her with me to Italy, to ski, with some friends of mine. Well, we were all ready to go and Teri didn't want to go, and she exploded with foul language. When she didn't want to do something she didn't want to do it. Period."

Pat remembered another time on Little Palm Island, where Teri worked at a resort for a while. "Teri was getting flirtatious with some of the men on the boat, and Charlie had to hold her back. But he didn't do it in an angry way. He was mellow, kind of slow." Everyone described Charlie as "slow." Slow and deliberate and with a vacant look in his eyes: It fits almost every description of every horror movie's bogeyman. One time, joking with Agent Dennis Haley, we compared Charlie to Michael Myers of *Halloween*, who never dies. Haley laughed and quipped back, "He reminds me more of Jason!" meaning the deranged murderer with the hockey mask on *Friday the 13th*. The following incident brings this image closer to a demonic reality.

"A SERIAL KILLER IS ON THE LOOSE"

The belief in a supernatural source of evil is not necessary: men alone are quite capable of every wickedness.

— Joseph Conrad

The experiences about to be described here may sound like so much nonsense or fairy dust to the incredulous, or even to the rational and sensible. Several people, however, witnessed them. And if some believe that the souls of some people who have died violently have not "crossed over to the light" and remain earthbound, explanations exist, albeit unsatisfactory to nonbelievers.

One reason: a spirit becomes attached to one or more living persons and wants to keep making contact. Thus, the phenomena of poltergeist experiences.

Gina Buell, who operates several of her family's restaurants in the Altamonte Springs area, was, at the time when this experience occurred, a young mother whose children attended a school owned and run by Debbie Knight, Michelle Jones's best friend.

Gina's mother, Gerry, is very good friends with British psychic Rosemary Altea, who has written several books.

"I was very skeptical," Gina said about psychic experiences. "But one time I was in college and was home for the summer, and decided I would go riding. My horse is really big, and he was very excited to go to the horse show. I went to the ring and was very apprehensive at first, and very nervous. Then suddenly a great calm came over me and, much to my surprise, I won all the riding awards. I came home and showed my trophies, and all of a sudden Rosemary looked to my left, and said, 'I know there is someone here who insists on talking to you.'" Rosemary told me the story of Romulus and Remus, the mythical founders of Rome who were cast into the Tiber River and rescued by a she-wolf, and I immediately knew who it was: my grandfather! He always used to tell me that story! Rosemary started talking about the horse show, and what I did right. Then she looked at me and said, 'I want you to stop beating yourself up.' When my grandfather was in the hospital I was a brat, and then he passed away. And I always felt so guilty."

One time, when Gina went back to her children's school, Debbie Knight told her she had had a death in the family. The next time Gina saw Debbie it was at a school meeting, and Rosemary Altea happened to be in town.

There was a school board meeting. "I was very insistent on going to the meeting," Gina said. "Something was dragging me there. When I saw Debbie, I gave her a hug."

Debbie had mentioned previously she thought there was something in her house, a presence that kept going up and down the steps on the stairs in her guesthouse.

"I said to Debbie, 'Could I see you outside for a minute? I understand you had a death in the family, but my mom's friend is a psychic medium.'" Debbie asked, "Can she come to my house?" Gina called her mother. Her mother asked Rosemary, and Rosemary said she would go to Debbie's house on a Saturday morning, at 8:00 a.m.

"I get there, and her husband is outside with the girls, and the girls could not get out of the house fast enough," Gina remembers.

Rosemary Altea has documented this encounter in her book, *A Matter of Life or Death.*

While the psychic was getting dressed, her guide, White Eagle, said, "This is more than you think." Once at the house, Debbie Knight said, "There's something here, in the guesthouse. My husband and my kids have seen it." And Gina noticed that it was freezing in the guesthouse.

"And it was the sunniest, brightest morning. There was also this awful smell in the place."

Rosemary walked past the kitchen, up the stairs, and into a room where there was a dining room table and love seat. "When Rosemary got in between the two bedrooms," Gina recounts. "She said, 'Right?' and she started taking off her jewelry. I was looking at my mom and asking her with my eyes, what is she doing? My mom smiled."

Rosemary had told the group that if she took off her jewelry, it meant there was a malignant presence and the energy would make her jewelry burn into her skin.

Gina continued her narration of the encounter: "So Rosemary said, 'Okay somebody's here.' Rosemary had me sit on the coffee-table Debbie was straight ahead, Rosemary to my left. And Rosemary said, 'This is what we're going to do. If you want to leave right now, don't scream or say anything. But if you stay, don't break the chain—we were holding hands. Rosemary started reciting the Hail Mary and Our Father. She said that my grandfather, her guide Gray Eagle, Debbie's mother and my grand-mother, who had both passed, and four angels were there. Rosemary started praying. Michelle kept trying to get into Rosemary. She went through exactly what happened in detail. I could hear Michelle through Rosemary. Rosemary's English accent was gone!"

Rosemary was narrating through all of this, and telling how Debbie had been over at Michelle's the night before.

By all accounts, Debbie had stayed the weekend at Michelle's house at Michelle's insistence that Debbie not drive if they were drinking. Debbie had stayed Friday and Saturday nights. She had gone to the kitchen on Saturday in the early morning hours to get a glass of water, and found Charlie pacing and pacing and pacing in the kitchen. She smiled and was slightly taken aback, and then Charlie stood over behind the kitchen counter, by the knives, and Debbie thought he was looking at her breasts. She felt so uncomfortable she left early Sunday morning.

Debbie had discussed this with Michelle, and said, "Your uncle is weird!" Michelle dismissed it, laughing and saying, "No, he's just a big teddy bear."

But back at Debbie's house, Gina remembered, "Debbie was crying so hard, her nose was running so hard, there was a puddle in her lap. I remember Michelle screaming; I was jumping out of my skin. Michelle was so angry, she was putting on the fight of her life. Rosemary was telling Michelle to go to her angels. There was a freaking battle going on in that room! The kitchen cabinets were opening and shutting, and someone was running up and down the stairs…Rosemary was telling him, 'You need to leave!' But he was telling her, 'I'm going to get her, and I'm going to get you.' Michelle was refusing to leave. My mom and I didn't know whether to leave. Rosemary was telling Michelle to go to her angels. Rosemary finally convinced her to go. Then, all of a sudden, the light came through the window, the stench was gone, and I thought I was crazy. I had to go to a birthday party for my son, and I was a basket case."

Rosemary Altea begins a chapter of her book: "There is a serial killer on the loose. A serial killer connected to at least 23 murders, and with the next victim already chosen."

She writes that the monster was all around, all-consuming. He said, "I'm going to get her, and then I'm going to get you." There was no doubt, Altea states: 'We were in the presence of the Devil."

Debbie was there, and so was Gina, and Gerry, Gina's mother. They all seemed to witness what went on.

Debbie and her husband Pat, whom she says is a non-believer, kept hearing footsteps going up and down the stairs of their guest home, which is adjacent to their own. Debbie had been having terrifying nightmares, and was convinced there was a presence in the house.

Rosemary heard her guide, Gray Eagle, say: "Pay attention; things are not as they might appear to be. Don't be complacent, Rosemary, don't be complacent."

The chapter from Altea's book states the psychic went to see Debbie on a Saturday morning. Debbie was shaking and crying and told Rosemary the whole story.

They went to the guesthouse, and Debbie and Gerry and Tina stood by the door. Altea explained the procedure in case there was an evil presence in the house. The guests would know if there was something wrong if Rosemary began taking off all of her jewelry. If she went into a trance state her energy could be strong enough that it would burn her skin if it came into contact with her jewelry.

She told Gerry, "If anything happens, just pray, and pray for light and angels…"

As she headed across the living room into the bedroom, wham! She felt as if someone had thrown a football, hard, right at her stomach.

Then the energy in the space went back to normal, but there was a sound.

Altea went back into the living room, took off all of her jewelry, and told the women that indeed there was a very malignant presence in the room. "Once we begin this, we must not leave until it's over. If I go into a trance it is very important we stay together in case I have to rely on your energy." And, she added, "in case there is a dark soul."

And then she realized Michelle had come to stand beside her friend Debbie. Gray Eagle was also there. The angels were there, but they had turned their backs. They would not interfere. The women, and whatever was there, were on their own.

Rosemary smiled at Michelle, but Michelle did not smile back. She was angry and afraid. "I knew instantly this young woman was in trouble." Rosemary then felt a very disgusting taste in her mouth, "like decaying, rotten meat. The monster was hiding." She felt the shadow was behind her, the same shadow Debbie and her husband shad seen moving through the house. Rosemary knew what Debbie had known all along:

that the shadow was Michelle's killer, and that Debbie was next.

Rosemary was the most dangerous one in the room for him, so he wanted to destroy her energy and diffuse her power. "The monster's ace card was fear...Negative energy made him strong. Michelle was full of anger, resentment, and fear." Debbie too, was resentful and fearful. "He was good, very good," Rosemary remembered.

Rosemary felt him trying to get into her mind. And she heard his voice, she writes, as an obscene, hoarse whisper: "I'm going to get you, and I'm going to get her too."

His plan had been to take Debbie and Michelle together.

"Not all killers are evil. Not all killers are dark souls, but Carl Brandt was a dark soul. Some would call him insane, but not me."

Both Michelle and Charlie were inside her, waging a battle. There were loud footsteps on the stairs. The shutters of the windows and the cabinet doors flung open; it was icy cold. This is what everyone present states they witnessed and felt.

"Get out! I am not afraid of you!" Rosemary shouted. And then, softly but firmly, she addressed the young dead woman: "Michelle, these are your choices. You can hold on to the monster and continue to be a victim, continue to give him power over you. If you do that, you will stay in that terrible dark place. Or you can look up; you can look to the light. Look to the light, Michelle, look to your angels. Let them take you to the light."

The room was now bathed in light, all present recount.

"You have no power over us, for your evil is useless here," Rosemary shouted to the entity she calls "the monster."

And then, Rosemary states, Michelle talked to Debbie. "Can you tell my mom that I'm okay? I'm with my angels. And Debbie, I will always be with you."

As for Debbie's state of mind after her best friend's brutal murder, and after the encounter, she wrote, and shared:

"Sick to my stomach.

Is this really happening?

I want to see my best friend again

Denial

Anger

Crying

Scared

Very, very scared!"

Why was Debbie so scared? A wife, a mother, a businesswoman who owns and runs a private school?

She explained:

"Shortly after Michelle's death, I became isolated from my family and friends. I never wanted to leave my house. I tried to keep my children home from school to be with me. Although physically there, I was checked-out emotionally, almost non-existent. My entire happy life as I once knew it was now in disarray; it was surreal. As weeks started to pass, I would start to encounter another very, very evil power…Charlie. I started to think I was crazy. I saw things, a lot of things that I wouldn't wish on my worst enemy. It was evil, it was dark; it was undeniably a part of my life I wish not to re-engage. He was lurking over me, haunting me and my home and bringing pain and an enormous amount of fear to me, every night. I saw things that no one should have ever seen; no one."

Debbie never discussed what "the things" that she saw were. About them, she has said: "I don't wish to open that door again."

She then speaks of a "specialist." "She came to my home and basically got rid of the evil spirits that plagued me. Since that visit, I have felt safe and although now our bedrooms and mainstay is in another part of my home (that was all in the guesthouse, before our main house was built), I still hear my family and friends who stay the night on occasion say that they have heard weird noises and have witnessed bizarre things in our guest home."

Apparently, to all present, Charlie, in whatever manifestation, was gone. And fortunately for her, Debbie sums up: "Eventually, over the years, things got better—never easier, just better."

Peggy Moore had a different, but somewhat similar experience.

"This happened about three weeks before the murders," Peggy, possibly the most levelheaded of Michelle's friends, recounted. Peggy Moore is a businesswoman who manages several properties. She has four children and does a lot of volunteering. She is hardly the sort of person who might fear spirits, or the beyond. Yet she was now admitting to some terrible premonitions.

"We had all agreed to meet one another at least once a month," she said of her close friends.

At this time, Peggy was living in the D.C. area with her husband, Joe, and in 2002 she agreed to fly in to Orlando to stay the weekend at Michelle's new house, which she had never seen.

"The minute I walked in I had this awful feeling," Peggy said. "It was oppressive, and I told Michelle, Debbie, and Lisa, who were there too. I told them, 'I feel awful! Like something very bad is going to happen here, something violent.'"

Michelle understood her friends, and tried to appease Peggy. "Sweetie, you are overworked," she told her. "Why don't you come in the hot tub with me and I will bring you a beer?" Peggy went in the hot tub, Michelle brought the beer, but Peggy states she did not feel any better. She got out.

Then, Michelle, now worried, tried to coax her: "Look, I got these new bed sheets and a down comforter. Why don't you lie down for a while?" Michelle then tried to offer an explanation to her friend. "Maybe it's because I took down the wallpaper in the kitchen and painted it mustard," she said. It was a desperate, last-minute attempt by Michelle to keep her friend Peggy staying for the weekend, as they had planned.

Peggy, not wanting to offend Michelle or say anything negative about her new house, a house her friend was so proud of, laid down for a while. Peggy did not think it was the kitchen's mustard paint that was getting her so out of sorts.

"I had to get up!" Peggy said. "I felt just awful! And I told them all again, 'I feel something violent is going to happen in this house. I cannot stay here!'"

The other girls were somewhat taken aback. This was not like Peggy, the rational mediator Peggy, who was always so intellectually inclined, and not prone to these outbursts at all, ever. But Peggy had to leave.

"I got in my car and went to my parents' house," Peggy said, adding that her parents were most surprised to see her, since they knew she planned on spending the weekend at Michelle's with the rest of the girls.

But being at her parents' home was not enough for Peggy at that point.

"I just had to get out of there, out of the entire area," she said. "I called my husband, Joe, and told him, 'I have to get out of here!' and he got me on the next flight back to D.C."

Once Peggy was back home, Michelle called her.

"You're not coming back, are you?" Michelle asked.

"No, Michelle," Peggy answered. "I'm not."

It was the last time Peggy saw her friend alive.

In his landmark book, *The Gift of Fear: Survival Signals that Protect Us from Violence,* author Gavin de Becker postulates that women have a certain instinct. "Theirs is viscerally named a 'gut feeling,' but it isn't just a feeling," De Becker explains. "It is a process more extraordinary and ultimately more logical in the natural order than the most fantastic computer calculations. It is our most complex cognitive process and at the same time the simplest.

"Intuition connects us to the natural world and to our nature. Freed from the bonds of judgment, married only to perception, it carries us to predictions we will later marvel at. 'Somehow I knew,' we will say about the chance meeting we predicted or about the unexpected phone call from a distant friend, or the unlikely turnaround in someone's behavior, or about the violence we steered clear of, or did not steer clear of. 'Somehow I knew...'"

Somehow, Peggy Moore knew.

Gale St. John is a psychic, a bona fide one. Larry King introduced her on his show as "the only psychic who has ever prevented a murder," and she did. She goes on searches with her cadaver dogs, for the missing and presumed dead. But she also gets answers from the world beyond. And members of law enforcement, as well as families of the disappeared, respect her.

This may again sound laughable to some people, but we have seen Gale in action, and one of us wrote her book, entitled *Blind Drive*. The title refer to the fact that when Gale goes searching, she does not want to know anything about the victim beforehand. And she drives through an area without knowing anything about it. She does not charge one penny for her services, except sometimes, if a place is far from her, for gas and lodging. It is her way of giving back. Her training with her dogs, border collies Kimber and Simon, is very arduous. Gale lives in Indiana, very close to Fort Wayne, where Charlie Brandt lived with his family in 1971, when he shot and killed his eight-month-pregnant mother and critically wounded his father.

Since Gale lives close to Fort Wayne, we asked if she would take a photo of Charlie's house for us. She said she would, and she did. And then she began to speak about Charlie.

For some reason, she said she'd begun to see him. She did not know who he was at all at the time, and did not know anything about this project. She said she'd perceived a foul smell of rotten fish.

Gale now despises Charlie. And she can be very humorous, with that dark humor that comes from dealing with death. One time, she said outright, "He is here; do you want to ask him anything?" The question was, through Gale: "Charlie, did you kill Carol Lynn Sullivan?" Again, Gale knew next to nothing about the case, let alone about Carol Lynn Sullivan, who remains a very guarded secret and not yet connected to Charlie. We even had to ask our colleague, Kathy Kelly, to dig up a couple of stories about the murder of Carol Lynn from the *Daytona Beach News-Journal* archives, it was so hidden.

Gale blurted out, "Oh, I hate him! Can you smack the dead? He is laughing and holding up the number thirteen!" Carol Lynn Sullivan had been about to turn thirteen when she vanished from her school bus stop. Gale did not know this, nor did she have the time to do any research on any of it.

Gale then added, "Oh, he is proud of all of this! He was proud when he killed his mother, and then he learned the system. And he has shown me absolutely no remorse. He is still a dark soul and he won't go." That was the way psychic Rosemary Altea had referred to Charlie too, as a "dark soul."

Then Gale said something significant: "He killed women with his eyes. He looked at women while thinking of the process of killing them."

This could be a psychological explanation for some of Teri's actions when Charlie and her marriage was becoming somewhat turbulent. Teri had wanted to call the sheriff on Charlie after she saw him covered in blood in the fish room; especially because, as she told Jim Graves, there had been a girl murdered nearby. Charlie's wife had wanted to move to the mainland, but did not. She was thinking of divorce, but she did not go through with it.

Was this part of the "anemic numbness" of which Dr. M. Scott Peck writes in his book, *People of the Lie*. Dr. Peck claims that the gradual effect of an evil person on a healthy person is exactly that: confusion and immobilization. Was it the "glazed-over look" that shrouded his wife with a blanket of inaction?

Perhaps for a few months before her murder, if not a year, Teri Brandt had been living in an alternate world, a world of Charlie's creation. She may have been living his reality. She certainly died by it.

DARLENE AND CAROL LYNN: NIGHT AND DAY

One was taken at dawn and the other in the shadow of night. The woman who was hooking in Little Havana was thirty-five. The twelve-year-old girl about to turn thirteen was waiting for her school bus.

September 20 was like any other Florida morning when Carol Lynn Sullivan woke up to a new day. Her mother, who acted as her alarm clock every morning, informed her it was time for her to get ready for school. The sun was shining through her bedroom window, and, like a lot of youths on the brink of breaking into their teenage years, Carol Lynn had a gnawing sense of independence brewing in her belly. She was eight days away from leaving the first twelve years behind. As she checked out her school clothes in the mirror and parted her hair down the middle, she faced the morning with a fresh sense of self. After breakfast, JoAnn Sullivan, got ready to walk Carol Lynn to her bus stop as she always had, and send her off to Deltona Junior High School. But this time, and from a new sense of pride rather than spite, which the girl never showed in her polite behavior, Carol Lynn emancipated herself for the day, exclaiming, "Mother, that's ridiculous! I'm grown up now!"

As Carol Lynn made her way out the front door to conquer the moderate walk to the bus stop, JoAnn smirked to herself as so many parents do when they see their little girl go off on her own for the first time. This is the brief period in a child-parent relationship in which this behavior is more humorous than harmful, and as any parent realizes upon self-reflection, they too had put their parents through the same routine. As JoAnn began the dishes she heard the front door close and let her mind wander back to the birthday party she had been planning for Carol Lynn's thirteenth birthday, and her entrance into young adulthood.

A few short minutes away a monster was breathing heavily, his eyes a piercing torch of terror, his intentions nothing short of destruction. In the early morning he had first seen the girl standing there, on the corner of Doyle Road and Courtland Boulevard, letting go of her mother's hand and stepping onto the yellow school bus. His obsession—an obsession that had consumed his life and destroyed so many others—was ignited, and for weeks he'd planned out his callous crime. Numerous times he had driven by, gazing with a glazed-over look, plotting and counting down the days until prey would fall victim to predator.

Now that day had come and just from behind the overgrowth on the corner he peered—waiting and watching. And then, there she was. A smile on her face, backpack over her shoulders, brown wavy hair parted down the middle. His pulse began to race and he could hardly contain himself. After a few moments she was within a mere couple of feet. Her back was to a vicious fate—one that could not stand to see innocence roam free.

On September 2, 1978, Carol Lynn Sullivan was standing alone waiting for her school bus at 7:00 a.m. She lived in Osteen, and the bus would take her to Deltona Junior High School. She never arrived at the school, and she was never seen again.

The Volusia County Sheriff's Department conducted extensive ground and air searches, to no avail.

His watch read 7:00 a.m. and just then, he saw two cars drive by. Using his hand as a makeshift muzzle, in a blitz-like fashion he came from behind the girl, covered her mouth, and dragged her back through the overgrowth and onto the other side in which he had meticulously placed his vehicle. After subduing the young Carol Lynn, he calmly drove back into society with the face of normalcy that had kept the beast within, masked for so many years. He did not take her back into his truck. He never took them outside; at least, not until 2004.

Eight days had gone by, and JoAnn Sullivan could only think one thing to herself: "I wish I would have driven her down." Carol Lynn's school had contacted her after Carol Lynn had not attended her first two classes that day, and JoAnn had called the authorities. This, combined with the twelve days since she had last seen her baby girl walk out the door, had been enough to make any parent worry, while enabling their worst nightmares to encompass their entire being. Then, on October 12, day twelve, just southwest of Doyle Road and Saxon Boulevard, about two miles from the bus stop, a fisherman trudging his way through a heavily wooded area near St. John's Lake stumbled upon the first major clue. Until this moment in the day his biggest worries had been how to fend off the oversized Florida mosquitoes constantly on the attack. It was just then, as his mind was elsewhere, that he'd noticed a rusted old paint can randomly lying at his feet. Unsure of its placement, yet curious of its contents, the fisherman pried open the can to find a human skull, badly decomposed, with only a small patch of hair remaining like a death flag raised high above its metal coffin.

When detectives were confronted with the find, they were baffled. None of them entertained the idea that the skull could have belonged to the Sullivan girl, since nature, and wildlife, had cleaned it clear of everything but the patch of hair.

Further searches were put in place to put an end to the mystery only leading to an answer to the question brought about by their suspicion. This was not the Sullivan girl, they thought.

The scene was an all-out assault by land, air, and sea. The galloping sounds of horse hooves ripping divots into the ground below were accompanied by the firing-up of alternators on the search engines known as four-wheelers. Dive teams infiltrated lakes and ponds searching for the slightest sight sign of bone, flesh, or discarded murder weapons. Through bubbles and murk they would spend hours searching only to come up short of anything other than suits plagued with bacteria from the warm Florida water. The sound of engines from the blades of a helicopter chopped its way through the air. Thorough as it was, the search produced nothing more than a team of people left utterly exhausted and frustrated. The skull would provide them with the way out of any further fruitless endeavors.

In a last ditch-effort, detectives had gone not only to Deltona Junior High School where Carol Lynn had attended, but also to South Seminole Middle School, where she had been a student the year before. They hit a dead end. A month would go by before an Orlando forensic odontologist would announce that Carol Lynn's dental records matched that of the skull found by the fisherman.

With all hopes demolished of finding the girl safe, attention was now focused on trying to paint a picture of the kind of person would commit such a heinous crime.

The few years leading up to the murder of Carol Lynn Sullivan had elicited more than suspicions that there might be someone out there abducting young women and snuffing out their lives. Local newspapers informed their readers that "some bodies have been found; others have never been heard from."

The sheriff on the case, Ed Duff, picked up the phone. On the other end was the voice of Dr. Walter McLaughlin, a Pennsylvania resident, retired FBI agent, and nationally renowned specialist in sex crimes.

This effort proved nothing more than another dead end in which the case became a mystery that would linger far longer than anyone involved could ever comprehend.

"The little girl was very obviously abducted, probably mutilated, even dissected," Sheriff Duff stated, not knowing those words would be the last hint at any resolution in the case of Carol Lynn Sullivan and what the paper deemed "probably Volusia County's most grisly unsolved murder in recent years."

And as he had so many times before, the monster walked away in the clear daylight while all eyes were diverted the other way.

Charlie's lifelong dream was to be a pilot. He wanted to go to Embry Riddle to do so, even with his juvenile record sealed, Embry Riddle said no. Was it Charlie who had killed the young girl? Was she his first?

JoAnn Sullivan cancelled the plans for Carol Lynn's thirteenth birthday. The Sullivans wanted answers after Charlie Brandt's murderous rampage in Central Florida. He did, after all, decapitate his victims.

Paul Crow, now retired Daytona Beach Chief of Police and then a homicide investigator for Volusia County, arrested a suspect whom he thought was likely to have committed the crime. His name was Wayne Earle Delisle. Delisle had stopped a car with a female driver inside it on Highway 11, beat her mercilessly and left her near death, and then took her out into a wooded area, took off her clothes, and stuck a knife in her genitalia. The woman survived and identified Delisle several times in photo lineups.

As to Carol Lynn Sullivan's manner of death, Crow points out Delisle was a pig farmer who boiled the heads of pigs to get the hair off. Delisle's "job" ar the sites of homes under construction was to pick up paint cans.

Crow even went so far as to take his unsolved crime, the murder of Carol Lynn Sullivan by Wayne Earle Delisle, to the FBI Headquarters in Quantico, Virginia, where he was one of a handful of detectives invited to take their profiling seminar.

"With the short timeframe, it appeared to them that the skull had been boiled," Crow stated of his colleagues at the Bureau. "People who are most involved in this practice come from a farm/ranch background. They boil pigs to remove the hair. I recognized he did come from that background. When I interviewed him he also mentioned that he removed empty paint cans from homes being developed, and sold them."

For his part, Carol Lynn Sullivan's father, Herbert Sullivan II, stated at the time, "Our family has waited for twenty years for an answer of some kind."

Carol Lynn Sullivan was one, among many, being investigated as victims of Charlie Brandt.

Herbert Sullivan held out hope.

"I think it's good, because we haven't heard anything in all these years. I mean, everything's been a deep silence for years. Nobody's ever given us anything substantial to go on, until now," he said.

Carol Lynn Sullivan's murder file remains among the cold cases.

Charlie Brandt has been twenty-one years old at the time of her murder.

If it holds true that serial killers never stop killing, and they don't— they usually move to another hunting ground, as Ted Bundy did, or are incarcerated or die first—young Carol Lynn Sullivan might have been Charlie's prey. "I think she was his first," Jim Graves said. Jim has never been able to forget his friend Charlie's demonic laughter at his mother's dinner table when Mrs. Graves was having both young men over for dinner and mentioned the girl's head in the paint can.

Dr. Michael Brannon believed Charlie did not ever stop.

"It is very likely there are other victims," said the forensic psychologist. "He had a predatory nature. Most murders are impulsive, but Brandt's murders are more like those of a predator hunting for a prey, or stalking a victim until the right opportunity or circumstances presented themselves. That behavior stays with a person. Although we don't know, we may assume that predatory behavior may have led to other murders. He would have no inhibitors. It is a rampant disregard for other people; it is like the killer has to dehumanize the victims somehow, in order to make themselves feel superior. It is almost like they deserve the fate that they get."

Edmund Kemper, "the Co-Ed Killer" took as his first victims, in 1972, Mary Anne Pesce and Anita Luchessa, both eighteen-year-old Stanford University freshmen. He beheaded them both. Eventually, the rest of Mary Anne Pesce's remains were found. Only Anita Luchessa's head was found.

Darlene Toler, a transplant from Michigan now living in Miami, should have been celebrating the day after Thanksgiving and looking towards Christmas with her three children and her boyfriend in the trailer park where they all lived.

But Darlene had to maintain a drug habit, a crack cocaine addiction, and sometimes went hooking along the seedier side of Eighth Street in Little Havana. She had been trying to turn her life around, but had been unsuccessful in that in Detroit, and relapsed time and time again.

Eighth Street is known as *Calle Ocho* in the heart of Little Havana. It's where its Latin residents celebrate Carnival Miami and the *Calle Ocho* Festival. But as it meanders further south and morphs into Tamiami Trail, it became sprinkled with cheap motels and traversed by prostitutes plying their trade in the night.

It was there, near the Rinker Cement Company, that Darlene Toler's body was found on the day after Thanksgiving, 1995. Miami Homicide Detective Pat Diaz now retired and turned private investigator, was called to the scene.

"Right after the murders of 2004 happened, they put out a press release across the state, looking for any cases that were similar," Diaz said. "They were aware of mine so there was immediate contact."

Diaz went to Charlie and Teri Brandt's house in Big Pine Key, and noticed Charlie kept pads with records of his mileage. Diaz looked at Thanksgiving Day of 1995, and he was certain this was his man. "There was a significant spike in his mileage," he noted. Then he noticed the anatomy chart behind the bedroom door.

"He left Darlene for us like a package, wrapped in a blanket inside a garbage bag, in pieces. He cut out her heart. Her head was never found." The experienced detective noticed the wounds the perpetrator had inflicted on his victim. "They were precise," he said. "He dissected her without cutting cartilage or anything; that's a skill."

When Diaz found out Charlie was an expert fisherman, that pretty much sealed the deal for him, except for one thing: the dog hairs found on the blanket in which Darlene Toler was wrapped before she was placed inside the garbage bag. Charlie and Teri did not have a dog—they had a cat.

Diaz would get his answer from Mary Lou Jones, Teri's sister and Michelle's mother.

"Melanie Fecher was Teri's best friend in Big Pine Key, one of the first people Teri met when she moved there," Mary Lou remembered. "Melanie and I had a number of conversations, when we were talking about that dog-hair business. Melanie and her husband Mark had spaniels and Charlie offered to take the dogs to the vet. "Teri worked in the daytime, and Charlie, he worked in the evenings," Mary Lou explained.

Melanie remembered that when she and her husband decided to move to Bradenton, Teri was at their house every night. "Teri was at my house crying every night when I was moving to Bradenton from the Keys," Melanie said. "In my mind I thought, no big deal, you'll come see me and I'll come see you." And the friends did visit, with Charlie and Teri making trips to Bradenton to see Teri's friend Melanie and her husband Mark, and Melanie and Mark driving down to Big Pine Key. That was, until 2004, the "Summer of Hurricanes," the summer of the murders.

"The last time Teri was supposed to come up, I was out playing golf and I couldn't even concentrate on golfing, I was so excited. I called her and said, 'At what time do you think you're coming? And she said, 'I don't know if we're coming; Charlie wants to see his dad.' I said, 'What? Charlie never sees his dad!' But she didn't say anything. And she didn't even invite me over to introduce me to them. I said, 'Okay, Teri, whatever,' and I hung up the phone. I still feel guilty over that." There seemed to be a lot of survival guilt going around over the murders of both Teri Helfrich Brandt and Michelle Jones.

And Melanie realized it was one of her dogs, since deceased, that tied Charlie to the gruesome murder of Darlene Toler in Miami.

"He was so good with my dogs," Melanie interjected, referring to her then-friend, Charlie Brandt. "One morning, I had to take my dog to the vet, and Charlie was very punctual about his job. But he called in to say he would be a little late and he took my dog to the vet."

Melanie Fecher, like so many others, only saw the mask of normality, except, again, for one incident.

Melanie told of a letter Charlie had written to her twelve years ago, in the year 2000.

"He wrote me a three-page love-letter telling me he was in love with me, and he wanted me, and wanted to be with me. He gave it to me before I went on vacation for two weeks. When I came back into town I said, 'I love you Charlie, and I also love Teri; I love her like a sister and you like a brother. You know there could never be anything between us.' But afterwards I was never alone with him again. For the longest time I had dreams of him chasing me and trying to kill me, and I would try to warn Teri and she wouldn't listen."

On the CBS *48 Hours* special "Deadly Obsession," Pat Diaz told correspondent Susan Spencer that he had wanted to have the dog hairs tested for DNA. "That would give me my hundred percent instead of my ninety-nine," he said.

Diaz eventually got his hundred percent. The dog hairs were tested. They were a match for Melanie and Mark Fecher's dog.

Like Teri Helfrich Brandt, Michelle Jones, Sherry Perisho, and possibly Carol Lynn Sullivan and others in Andros Island and around Florida, and even as far as Germany and Holland, Darlene Toler, for completely different reasons than the other women, didn't stand a chance.

Laura Welch is Darlene's sister-in-law, married to Darlene's brother, who had since passed away from cancer.

Darlene had moved to Florida ten years before her murder to hopefully begin a new life she says.

Darlene's mother, Betty Jo, worked in a bar, and all her five children had different fathers. "My sister-in-law said she did what she did to take care of her three children," Welch said. "My mother-in-law told me, while she was living, that she had made a lot of mistakes. And, sure enough, one of her girls died young from being obese, and the other four were drug addicts." Darlene was the second-oldest, and little did Betty Jo knew, or her brother or sister-in-law the fate that awaited her on that dark thoroughfare on Tamiami Trail.

"She'd hook when she needed drugs, and then she'd get clean and then go back," Laura remembered of her sister-in-law when she was still in Detroit.

Darlene's boyfriend worked as a butcher at a Cuban grocery store during the day, and cared for her children at night, when she went hooking. According to Laura, he was a good man who cared for Darlene and the kids. "Of course, the whole family thought the boyfriend did it, including my brother. He was Cuban and they were all very racist."

But Darlene's boyfriend was not the culprit. It was another butcher: a fisherman, who loved cutting up his catch while it was still alive; who studied anatomy, and even kept a diagram of a human heart inside his *Gray's Anatomy* book, who was obsessed with body parts, and killing and disemboweling women, who had killed and disemboweled Darlene Toler and left her on the side of the Tamiami Trail in Miami "like a package."

Pat Diaz believes the killer of Darlene Toler and the others was evil. "Absolutely!" he said. "He never got rehabilitation. That rage stayed with him as part of his life. He had deep dark secrets."

But at least Darlene Toler's murder and disembowelment would not remain a secret.

The murders of Teri Helfrich Brandt and Michelle Jones in Orlando would lead investigators back to both Toler and Sherry Perisho.

What follows is the police report of the investigation, and the conclusions to both murders, which are now closed:

On September 1, 2005, Special Agent Leslie D'Ambrosia was contacted by Detective Rob Hemmert of the Seminole County Sheriff's Office concerning the homicides of Michelle Lynn Jones and Teresa Brandt committed by Carl Brandt prior to his committing suicide.

Detective Rob Hemmert advised that the DNA analysis indicated that Carl "Charlie" Brandt's DNA was identified in the rectal area of victim Michelle Jones.

On October 7, 2004, Special Agent Leslie D'Ambrosia consulted with Detective Pat Diaz of the Miami-Dade Police Department, Homicide Bureau, concerning the unsolved homicide of Darlene Toler.

In November 1995, the remains of Darlene Toler were discovered along the roadside in western Miami-Dade County. Toler had been wrapped in a shower curtain that was secured with cord.

Her head and heart had been removed with a cutting instrument. Neither has been recovered.

Toler was last seen in the City of Miami several miles east. She was a known prostitute and narcotics user.

SA D'Ambrosia and Det. Diaz discussed the possible linkage of the Toler homicide to the Perisho, Brandt and Jones homicides. Det. Diaz further advised that he possessed information on several homicides involving prostitutes in Miami-Dade and Broward Counties that necessitated a review and analysis for linkage puposes.

Mark Coleman Monroe County Sheriff's Office

Detective Corey Bryan Monroe County Sheriff's Office

Investigator Rob Hemmert Seminole County Sheriff's Office

Investigator Robert Jaynes Seminole County Sheriff's Office

Investigator Mark Smeester Escambia County Sheriff's Office

Detective Sergeant Jim Van Allen Ontario Provincial Police

Dr. Peter Collins Ontario Provincial Police

Sergeant Eric Latour Quebec Provincial Police

At the conclusion of the consultation, an opinion was offered that it was likely that Carl Brandt was responsible for the murders of Sherry Perisho in Big Pine Key in 1989 and of Darlene Toler in Miami-Dade County in 1995.

This opinion was based on the similar crime details and their indication of a signature behavior involving the cutting and removal of the victims' hearts and heads.

Signature behaviors are unique and are an integral part of the offender's behavior that go beyond the actions needed to commit the crime.

As offenders fantasize about their crimes, they develop a need to ex-

press their violent fantasies.

When they are finally acted out, the totality of some aspects of the crime demonstrate a unique personal expression, or ritual, based on these fantasies.

When committing the crime does not satisfy the offender, this insufficiency compels him or her to go beyond the scope of the offense to perform a ritual. Any ritual displayed at the crime scene is the offender's signature aspect. In the homicides of Sherry Perisho and Darlene Toler, the signature included the removal, or attempted removal of the head and the heart of his victims, as well as the unique methodology utilized. Additionally, the method of removal was similar in both cases to Carl Brandt's known murder of Michelle Jones in Seminole County in 2004.

Although there are historical cases involving organ removal or decapitation it is rare to have both the heart and head removed at the same time.

In the case of Jessica Schuchman in Escambia County in 2001, her body was found dismembered on a beach near the US Naval Base and appeared to have been in the water for a short period of time.

Other body parts were recovered on another beachfront. It was determined by analyzing the crime-scene details that the offender removed the victim's limbs, but did not attempt to cut the torso or remove the heart, or any other organ. The offender in this case also did not make any attempt to remove the victim's head.

Since the offender would have spent a considerable amount of time cutting the limbs from the victim's body, it would be expected that he would have had the time to remove the heart and/or head of this victim as well.

It would be expected that, since time was not an issue to this offender, he would have engaged in those behaviors that were gratifying to him, specifically those signature aspects seen in the linked homicides.

In this case it was more likely that the victim was dismembered for transportation and disposal purposes.

The opinion was offered that the Schuchman homicide was not related to Perisho, Toler, or Jones.

Charlie Brandt had not raped any of his other victims.

As to why he sodomized Michelle Jones after she was dead, Special Agent and profiler Leslie D'Ambrosia states:

"It was the ultimate desire for him, and since he knew he could not get away with it, he chose to commit these acts and kill himself. Obsessive sexual fantasy wins over the reality of consequences. He thought this out. He pretty much said goodbye to his dad when he visited him."

Herbert Brandt had thought during Charlie's last visit to him, right before he and Teri headed out to Michelle's home in Altamonte Springs, that Charlie had held him tighter than he ever had, as if saying good-bye for the last time.

OTHER CRIMES?

This information is from another police report from the Florida Department of Law Enforcement.

n October 8, 2004, Special Agent Leslie D'Ambrosia and Special Agent Tom Davis, FDLE Melbourne Office, discussed possible linkage analysis of several cases involving subject Carl Eric Brandt, who murdered his wife and niece in September 2004.

SA D'Ambrosia advised that crime scene reports, autopsy reports and photographs were needed to complete an analysis of some unsolved homicide, possibly committed by Brandt.

SA Davis advised that he would obtain the necessary information for analysis from the Seminole County Sheriff's Office. Additionally he advised that he would be constructing a timeline of Brandt's whereabouts from data/documents seized from the Brandt residence.

This report is in conjunction with the ongoing investigation into a series of homicides committed throughout the State of Florida, which may be related to two homicides committed by Carl Eric Brandt in Seminole County, Florida, in September 2004. Brandt hung himself following the murders of his wife and his wife's niece.

On October 13, 2004, Special Agent Leslie D'Ambrosia contacted Detective Sgt. Jim Van Allen of the Ontario Provincial Police in Orillia, Canada. SA D'Ambrosia requested a query of the Canadian ViCLAS system to determine if any homicide had been reported involving the removal of a victim's heart.

On October 14, 2004, Det. Sgt. Van Allen advised that a query of over 160,000 cases was conducted country-wide. There were no reported unsolved cases involving the removal of a heart.

Although investigators, especially the Canadian police, are basing Charlie Brandt's linkage to the crimes there on the removal of the hearts, is it not possible that at some point Charlie changed his signature, either at random or to escape detection?

Nobody will ever know.

What follows are the cold crimes that could, or could not, be connected to Carl "Charlie" Brandt:

CAROL LYNN SULLIVAN (Could be connected to Charlie Brandt)

On September 20th, 1978, Carol Sullivan left her residence en route to her bus stop on Doyle Rd. near Courtland Blvd. in Deltona, FL. and was never seen alive again. Several days later her remains were found. (Charlie would have been 21 and it might have been his first crime.)

MARY LOUISE REDDICK (Before Teri's diary, and when Charlie was in the Daytona area.)

On February 10th, 1979 Mary Reddick's body was found near the intersection of Green St. and S. Delaware Ave., in Deland, FL. Her body showed signs of violent trauma and her death was ruled a homicide.

JANE DOE #1 (This crime may have been committed by Gerald Stano or Charlie Brandt while they were both working in the Daytona area)

On November 5th, 1980, the skeletal remains of a deceased white female, approximately 18—25 years of age, approximately 5'-8" tall, brown hair, and approximately 124—135 lbs., were found on MM 257 SB, I-95 side approximately one mile north of Taylor Rd., Port Orange, FL. The remains showed signs of violent trauma and her death was ruled a homicide.

PAMELA SUE JONES (Before Teri's diary and when Charlie was in Daytona)

On December 12th, 1980, Pamela Jones's body was found in a wooded area near Howard St. and Courtland Blvd., in Deltona, FL. Jones was known to frequent the Daytona Beach area and was believed to be from

Indiana. Her body showed signs of violent trauma and her death was ruled a homicide.

ON DECEMBER 9TH, 1988, TERI REPORTED THEY CLOSED THE DEAL ON THEIR HOUSE ON BIG PINE KEY; THIS FACT HELPS GIVE PERSPECTIVE ON THE NEXT GROUP OF CASES.

DENISE DANSBY

In May of 1989, Denise Dansby arrived in Volusia County from Texas and checked into a motel in Daytona Beach Shores, FL. Her family reported her missing on June 12th, 1989. Days later her rental car was located but Dansby was not located.

On December 9th, 1989, Dansby's skeletal remains were found off of Osteen Cemetery Rd., Osteen, FL. The remains showed signs of violent trauma and the death was ruled a homicide.

TERI'S DIARY AT THAT TIME: April 27th till May 7th—both she and Charlie go to New Orleans, LA.

May 8—weird day

June 7 till June 10th—Teri goes to Ft. Lauderdale, FL

July 11—rough conversation

June 12th—Denise Dansby's family reported her missing, which means they were used to hearing from her frequently and hadn't for a brief amount of time.

Teri Helfrich Brandt was gone for three of the five days leading up to them filing this report.

JANE DOE #2

On April 23rd, 1990, the skeletal remains of a white female were found in a wooded area east of Clyde Morris Blvd., and 1.5 miles north of Strickland Range Rd., Daytona Beach, FL.

The victim was killed approximately 3—8 weeks prior to being discovered. The victim was approximately 5'-4" tall, medium build, brown hair in pigtails with red bands, extensive dental work with unusual teeth.

Teri reports that both she and Charlie were in West Palm Beach from March 15th to March 17th. From April 26th till May 1st they were in Ft. Walton Beach, FL.

ZOE ANNA GUMBY

On August 8th, 1990, the body of Zoe Gumby was found in a wooded lot on Walker St. in New Smyrna Beach, FL. Gumby's body showed signs of violent trauma and her death was ruled a homicide.

(Teri's planner shows nothing about their whereabouts at this exact time. Closest date noted is from July 6th till July 9th when they were in Homestead, Vanderbilt Beach, and Sanibel, FL. From October 12th till October 16th Teri in Boston, at a family reunion.)

JANE DOE #3

On August 19th, 1991, the remains of an unidentified female were discovered in the area of Little Lake in Osteen, FL. The remains showed signs of violent trauma and the death was ruled a homicide.

(Teri reports that on July 22nd, Charlie got no contract news, and that on August 13th it was a "weird day, rough, runaway [sic] and hide feeling." Three days, there may be a stressor.)

LARALEE SPEAR

On April 25th, 1994, Laralee Spear was reported missing by her family after she failed to return home from DeLand High School. The victim's body was located in a secluded area behind a home on Deerfoot Rd., DeLand, FL. The remains showed signs of violent trauma and the death was ruled a homicide.

(Teri reports that they were in the Bahamas from March 1st until March 4th then says nothing till May 31st. Open ended.)

MYRTLE REXROAD

On May 6th, 1997, the victim was found deceased under the I-4 overpass off of Old Deland Rd. in DeBary, FL. Upon autopsy of Rexroad, her death was ruled as a homicide.

(Teri's reports in her planner note no more than the fact that January 1 was very emotional, and that from September 9 till September 17 they were in California. But Teri had been, at that time, alone in California, attending another family reunion.)

THE MAKING OF A
SERIAL KILLER

n January, 2006, two years after the murders of Teri Brandt and Michelle Jones, the Fort Wayne, Indiana newspaper *The Journal Gazette* published a two-part series entitled "The Darkness in Charlie." Reporter Ron Shawgo wrote the story, defining it with this slugline:

"Carl 'Charlie' Brandt never explained why. And what he started here 35 years ago may always remain a mystery."

It probably will remain a mystery. Charlie is no longer around to explain it, or divlulge as Ted Bundy wanted to do in a last-ditch effort to postpone his execution for yet another round. Charlie, con man that he was, probably would have.

Ilse Brandt, Charlie's mother, has long been dead at her son's hands, and both his father, Herbert Brandt, and Angela Brandt, his older sister and the only other living relative with any memories of him, have refused all requests for interviews. The two younger sisters had no prior knowledge of their mother's murder, and were always told their mother had died in a car accident. They, of course, do not remember anything. Herbert and Angela Brandt not only refused an interview with CBS' *48 Hours*, but were unreachable for this book as well. Herbert's phone at his residence in Ormond Beach has the message: "This number is not available for incoming calls." Angela's number in St. Augustine, her last recorded address, has been disconnected. "Maybe she doesn't want to be found," her ex-husband, Jim Graves, commented.

After the suicide/murders, Angela told the police she was glad Charlie was dead. She had been afraid of him all of those years following their mother's murder. Even in the Florida heat, she would shut off her air-conditioner, close the windows, and lock them. It is not unlikely she would still be afraid of her brother's past, like a family curse, were he still alive. And she might be afraid he would come back.

Donald Withers remembers that when Angie was married to Dave, and Angie and Dave and Donald were hanging out, Angie had said on a few different occasions that when she had moved in with Jim after living with Charlie, she'd had trouble sleeping. "She was worried Charlie was going to come over, and scared of how Charlie was going to take her moving out." Donald just took it to mean that Angie was worried Charlie would be upset that she'd moved out, but not worried to the extreme that he now knew.

For his part, retired detective Pat Diaz thinks that "it all goes back to the mother." Perhaps the private investigator, with twenty-six years experience as a homicide detective in Miami, was subscribing to the Freudian account of matricide; a boy's early Oedipal relationship with his mother would engender such a love-and-hate dichotomy.

What is known, according to Charlie's statement to psychiatrists, is that his mother "nagged him too much."

Speaking to investigators after Charlie had murdered his mother, Charlie's father said: "He's a good kid. He was just having a bad day." A bad day? A kid might have a bad day and go for a walk and slap some trees with a stick, or smash his model airplane; but kill his eight-month-old pregnant mother?

Perhaps in part it did "go back to his mother," as Pat Diaz concluded. But what about his father?

Angela Brandt had told Jim Graves, when they were married and when she first told her husband about her brother's past, that their father Herbert was born in Germany—as was their mother—and that Herbert had belonged to the Hitler Youth.

It is worthwhile and apropos here to take a look at this phenomenon, part of one of the most nefarious and deadly regimes in history:

"My program for educating youth is hard. Weakness must be hammered away. In my castles of the Teutonic Order a youth will grow up before which the world will tremble. I want a brutal, domineering, fearless, cruel youth. Youth must be all that. It must bear pain. There must be nothing weak and gentle about it. The free, splendid beast of prey must once again flash from its eyes....That is how I will eradicate thousands of years of human domestication....That is how I will create the New Order." — Adolf Hitler, 1933.

Twenty-three years of a rampant ideology of xenophobia and extermination had finally come to an end in 1945. In September, 1944, one year before the end—yet in year six of World War II—Hitler Youth Leader Artur Axmann spewed these words:

"As the sixth year of war begins, Adolf Hitler's youth stand to fight resolutely and with dedication for the freedom of their lives and their future. We say to them: You must decide whether you want to be the last of an unworthy race despised by future generations, or whether you want to be part of a new time, marvelous beyond all imagination." Herbert Brandt, according to the timeline, was already enlisted in the Hitler Youth camps.

It was 1922 when the Hitler jugend or Hitler Youth was formed. Created to be a paramilitary organization for the Nazi party, it was composed of two sections. Males fourteen or older would go on to comprise the Hitlerjugend proper, while those younger would build the Deutsches Jungvolk section. (This section didn't come into fruition until 1930.)

The organization was set up with nothing more than the intention to turn the children into faithful defenders of the anti-Semitic doctrine, creating future soldiers who would go blindly into battle without truly understanding the big picture of what the Third Reich was trying to accomplish. The common reading material amongst the youths were monthly magazines entitled *Wille und Macht* (Will and Power) and *Die*

Kameradschaft (Comradeship), and a yearbook called *Jungen eure Welt* (Youth: Your World).

The original mission of the Hitler Youth was to instill strict loyalty to Nazi doctrine and to bring Hitler to power. With those missions accomplished, the youths began to find the routines of attending weekly meetings a drag, and as of 1936, the whole program had hit a stagnant wall. When the war began in September of 1939, a second wind had hit the organization and the youths felt revitalized with a new sense of purpose. They handed out draft cards, collected scrap metal and other war materials, and delivered ration cards while acting as impromptu postmen. As the war progressed, they were instructed to man antiaircraft batteries. Having flak guns stationed near their homes kept them in the battle, but saved them from having to travel. Not long after the implementation of the flak guns, youths ended up being sent all over Germany. Jobs included operating searchlights and riding their bikes around dispatching communication, all the while at risk of losing their lives to incoming bombs. After bombing had commenced, youths would take part in the cleanup crew and funnel civilians into new living locations.

At the peak of the Hitler Youth movement, the membership count was at 8.8 million. One of the young boys partaking in these activities and making up this figure was Herbert Brandt.

Born in 1931, he would have been recruited by the Deutsches Jungvolk around 1941. The exact specifics of what he did and did not do, we do not know. Whether he truly bought into the ideology of the Nazi movement or was just doing as he was told, we also will never know for sure. The only clue is a possible coincidence (or not?) that Herbert would later name his first son Carl Brandt. Why would this be a clue? Karl Brandt was a well-known member of the Nazi movement who acted as Hitler's personal physician while co-heading the Euthanasia Program. This is someone Herbert would have known about as a boy.

Psychiatrists were baffled by the murder of his mother and the serious wounding of his father by thirteen-year-old Charlie. It is possible that neither the young Charlie nor the adult Charlie were ever able to understand the reasons for his desire to kill.

But if Ilse, Charlie's mother, "nagged him too much," Herbert, his father, had to be a strict disciplinarian, according to his background.

Psychologist Michael Brannon concurred:

"From that sort of background and indoctrination, and what we know about it, we can assume those people would grow up to be less empathetic of other people, and of how their behavior would impact someone else. They would feel superior to others, and this would interfere with their feeling remorse." That was precisely the goal of Hitler's and the Third Reich's indoctrination and programming.

Many seem to want to attach the label "stressor" to the shooting of the family dog by Herbert. Charlie said the dog was everybody's pet, but he had become very attached to the beagle. The Brandts had only been home less than twenty-four hours after they returned to Fort Wayne from their vacation in Florida, where Herbert had taken Charlie hunting and shot the dog by mistake, he said.

Charlie's father explained to the officers that the dog had run away the day before, so they'd had to go back and look for him the next day. The dog never obeyed commands, which made Herbert angry. And he was angrier still that the dog wouldn't come out of the bushes. So, he claimed, he shot at the bushes to scare him out, and accidentally shot and killed him.

The natural explanation for Charlie's act would have been a reaction to losing his best friend at the hands of his father. However, that wasn't what he told police.

When an investigator asked him, "What did you say to your dad when he shot the dog?" Charlie responded: "I didn't think that he would do it. I heard two shots. He just didn't say anything. I asked him if he missed him 'cause I didn't see anything. I wanted to cry but I stopped myself, and we just kept on hunting for the last few hours."

If Charlie wanted to cry, why didn't he? Because the tears would not come, or because of Herbert's disciplinary attitude? And how could he have kept on hunting animals with his father after his beloved dog had been shot dead?

Less than a week after the shooting of his mother, two experts determined that Charlie had no mental disabilities. One told a judge that Charlie should not be placed in jail or a hospital.

The other said Charlie had acted on an irresistible impulse and had a moral, not mental, defect.

When he answered the police officer's question as to why he'd originally gotten the gun to inflict damage on his parents, Charlie replied, quietly, "It was like I was programmed." He had not wanted to do that, he said. He "loved" his family.

From the county jail, where he was placed for a few months, Charlie attended his mother's funeral in shackles. By all accounts, he expressed neither remorse nor sorrow.

A Fort Wayne grand jury had cautioned that thirteen-year-old Charlie might kill again if he did not receive the proper therapy. Did he?

There was a precedent to Charlie's juvenile barrage on his parents, but on the other side of the country, in California, where a monster who later received the moniker "the Co-ed Killer" was born, and where he carried out his deadly rampage.

On August 27, 1964, seven years before Charlie Brandt murdered his mother, fifteen-year-old Edmund Kemper was living at the seventy-acre home of his paternal grandparents in North Fork, California. Already an imposing figure at six-foot-four, the shy and awkward teen was deemed a problem by both his father and his mother, the latter of whom he despised. His grandmother was equally strict. As an adult, Kemper would describe himself as a "walking time bomb" on account of his anger. This was turned into inner rage by the disparaging treatment of his mother and then his grandmother, both of whom seemed to do nothing but give him orders in shrill, admonishing voices.

In *Murder and Madness,* psychiatrist Donald Lunde states that as a child, Kemper had fantasies about killing and mutilating women. In fact, he wished everyone in the world would die, and he wanted to kill them himself. On that August afternoon, he argued loudly with his sixty-year-old grandmother, Maude. Dr. Lunde, who was able to interview Kemper at length in later years, states that the boy projected his rage at his mother onto his grandmother. He took a rifle, and when his grandmother yelled at him not to shoot the birds, he shot her instead, twice in the back, then stabbed her with a kitchen knife.

Like Charlie's, Edmund's was an impulsive act, and not premeditated—although Charlie had sat at the dining-room table doing his homework with his father's Luger concealed. How could young Kemper hide from his kindly grandfather the murder of his wife at her grandson's hands? It was his own seventy-two-year-old grandfather, also named Edmund, who had given his grandson the twenty-two caliber gun the previous Christmas.

The first order of business for the big kid was to hide the grandmother's corpse in the bedroom. With his size and strength, he had no problem dragging the lifeless old woman there.

Then, as his grandfather drove up to the front of the house, young Kemper went to the window, trained his rifle on the older man, and shot him dead.

At age fifteen, Kemper was committed to the Atascadero State Hospital, where he befriended his psychologist and even became his assistant. Tests during his time at Atascadero revealed that he had an I.Q. of 136. Later, during adulthood, he tested at 145. Kemper was released from prison in 1969, after serving fewer than five years. At the time of his release, he had grown to 6 feet 9 inches and weighed close to 280 pounds. Against the wishes of several doctors at the hospital, he was released into his mother's care.

Young Kemper wanted to go into law enforcement, but was not admitted into the police academy because of his height. However, he did frequent a bar that was a favorite watering hole of the local cops, and befriended many of them. They drank together, and Kemper was jovial and told jokes. The officers thought of him as a "gentle giant" until Kemper killed and dismembered six female college hitchhikers in the Santa Cruz area. Once the women got into his car, they were his, he stated. Kemper severed the heads of his victims, and engaged in necrophilic acts with their corpses. After that rampage, he went back home and butchered his own mother. He wanted to throw her vocal cords in the garbage disposal, to ultimately destroy the source of his torment, but was unable to. He then brought his mother's best friend and neighbor over to the house, and choked her to death from behind so she couldn't act as a witness.

Finally, he called the cops, his friends who drank with him and liked him. The officers thought he was joking until he gave a detailed confession. He is currently serving a life sentence, and is a model prisoner.

There is a prevailing feeling among people that violent juvenile offenders can be rehabilitated, and that life in prison is too harsh for teens.

An article published by the *Associated Press* on Monday, June 25, 2012 reported that the Supreme Court had ruled it unconstitutional to sentence juveniles to life in prison without parole for murder.

The decision came in the robbery and murder cases of Evan Miller and Kuntrell Jackson. Miller was convicted in 2006 of capital murder for beating a man with a baseball bat and leaving him to die in a burning trailer after stealing his baseball card collection and $350. The killing occurred in 2003.

Miller's co-defendant testified against him in exchange for a lighter sentence for his own murder, robbery and arson charges.

Colby A. Smith testified that he and Miller, who was 14 at the time of the murder, decided to kill Cole Cannon for money, according to reports from the sentencing. Smith testified that after he hit Cannon with a bat, Miller began bashing the victim with the bat and said: "Cole, I'm God and I've come to take your life." They later set fire to his trailer, where the man's remains were discovered.

The Alabama Court of Criminal Appeals upheld the sentence on the grounds that Miller's sentence was not overly harsh when compared to his crime, a ruling the Supreme Court disagreed with.

"No one can doubt that (Miller) and Smith committed a vicious murder," Justice Elena Kagan said in the court's ruling. "But they did it when high on drugs and alcohol consumed with the adult victim. And if ever a pathological background might have contributed to a 14-year-old's commission of a crime, it is here."

No doubt this is the subject of endless debates, and one might find oneself on the fence in that respect, but what about the expunging of records of violent juvenile offenders? In this case, the laws vary from state to state, and there is nothing definitive in the books as of yet.

Charlie's father was in critical care from his wounds, but recovered. Charlie was interviewed by a psychiatrist, a Dr. Green, who went to visit him. He described the day of the murder. Dr. Green's assessment was that the youngster fit no particular diagnostic category for mental illness. Charlie had acted impulsively, the psychiatrist said, being a "victim of ill-defined impulses." It was his opinion that Charlie was suffering from an uncontrollable impulse but was competent. The same had been said of Edmund Kemper.

At the Allen County Jail, Charlie was evaluated by a psychologist, a Dr. Heineman, who said he had a schizoid personality. Another psychiatrist, Dr. Ronald Pancner, saw him on two different occasions. Charlie told Dr. Pancner that he didn't have any trouble with his parents, but didn't like school. He liked to be home, and liked to be by himself. The family had just moved to Fort Wayne from Connecticut, where Charlie had had friends in school. He didn't like it in Indiana, he said. His EKG showed no abnormality, no health problems. Charlie was, for all intents and purposes, a normal thirteen-year-old boy.

In May, 1971 the Department of Mental Health moved him to Central State Hospital in Indianapolis. He was officially admitted on May 25. until June 16 of 1972.

West of downtown Indianapolis, reaching to West Washington Street, there are ten cold, institutional-looking brick buildings, spread out over 160 acres of land. This is also the address of the Indianapolis Medical History Musem. There are daily tours given, and people from all over attend to have a one-on-one with the dinosaurs of mental illness past. Here 146 years ago was the grand opening for the Indiana Hospital for the Insane, and the famous Kirkbridge architectural setup.

The facilities had unfit bedding, improper staff training, lack of heat, lack of light, and cockroaches running through the kitchens. In 1883, under the supervision of Superintendent Richard Fletcher, Dr. Sarah Stockton was hired and became the first recognized female doctor in Indiana and one of only twenty-two female doctors in the United States. Superintendent Fletcher continued to make bold moves to implement reforms for the hospital and to provide dignity and respect for the patients, including publicly burning restraints and banning the anonymous burials of patients who had succumbed to death.

In 1896, the hospital achieved another first under the mandate of Superintendent George Edenharter, by installing the very first pathology laboratories in the United States. At the same time, the world of criminology was plowing headfirst into new territory through the work of Dr. Max Bahr, who was spearheading studies into the links between crime and mental illness. During this time, the hospital would change the name on the marquee from "Central State Indiana Hospital for the Insane," to simply "Central State Indiana Hospital," and Dr. Bahr would create some of the first forensic psychiatric courses that would be taken by American lawyers.

The 1950's saw the downfall of the hospital.

All that time pharmaceutical companies began to concoct drugs that could help patients with retardation and other controllable conditions. The patients under those categories were thrown into halfway houses or smaller hospitals, while the more serious cases remained at Central State. Because of this new scientific breakthrough in the legal-drug world, the population at the hospital dropped significantly and laid the groundwork for the eventual disposal of the world occupied by both the insane and the sane.

By the mid-1960's, the quality of care had diminished to frighteningly pathetic lows. Clifford Williams, who ruled as superintendent at the time, reported there only being one bathtub and three toilets to service all twenty-four wards.

It would be 1971 when Charlie would see the inside of the asylum walls, walls that would hold so many screams and cries and hide deplorable situations that, frighteningly enough, he may have found comfortable or comforting. He never complained about it. It was a place where he would learn and practice the art of manipulation, and with doctors' recommendations, he would be on the outside looking in, walking free and back into society, in just a year.

During his hospitalization, he presented a very mild persona. He wasn't argumentative, and his initial assessment showed only an adjustment reaction. He was seen by psychologists and social workers, but was able to go home on weekends. He was given individual psychotherapy. He attended his group therapy and participated. A social worker commented that he did not want to talk about his mother, and never gave them any clue as to why he shot her.

The youngster only made one deprecating comment about his mother. He said she "nagged him," and that when he complained, "she hollered a lot."

After the Christmas holiday he participated more in group therapy. He went to high school while in the mental hospital, but while there, he would just listen and not participate. This was a pattern that would continue later in life. Friends of Michelle Jones all commented that at gatherings, Charlie was attentive to Teri, seemingly to avoid participating in the goings-on.

At the hospital, he played basketball with other inmates, though he said he didn't want to. He became a model patient. He knew he had to conform and to fly under the radar to do what he wanted to do.

Later, he would tell his older sister, Angela, "I knew when they wanted me to cry, so I did." Charlie was learning how to mimic human behavior—how to be quiet, how to fit in, how to be a model patient, and how to appear a good friend and an ideal husband. In a word, he wanted to seem normal. Over time, he would strive for outward perfection.

When Detective Rob Hemmert interviewed his father, the investigator noticed that Herbert Brandt appeared authoritative and very rigid.

For her part, Mary Lou Jones, a psychiatric nurse, states: "I think there was something about his mother and his father that was extremely controlling."

Michelle Jones's mother did not elaborate. It was just something she sensed, she said.

Charlie remained at the hospital in Indiana for a year.

If a love-hate relationship with his mother is the breeding ground for a potential serial killer, perhaps both Detective Pat Diaz and Mary Lou Jones were right. Did Ilse Brandt draw Charlie close, perhaps too close, to then admonish him in turn for something as simple as not doing his homework? No one will ever know.

Dr. Michael Brannon is a forensic psychologist, often asked to give expert testimony in criminal trials, and who also has appeared on the Investigative Discovery Channel as a crime consultant.

Dr. Brannon said he believes Charlie was already predisposed to engage in antisocial behavior. "We do know that there are positional as well as situational factors to this behavior," he stated, "because circumstances may play a part as to how they act out that behavior. But I believe something was festering in him for some time, not just during the course of that day." There had to be, for Charlie to have gone upstairs to the nightstand, gotten his father's Luger, and concealed it as he did his homework in the kitchen before walking upstairs and beginning his deadly rampage on his own family.

During the CBS *48 Hours* episode, "Deadly Obsession," about the murders of Michelle Jones and Teri Brandt, correspondent Susan Spencer interviewed Dr. Ronald Pancner and asked him several questions about Charlie's mental health, to which the psychiatrist replied that his patient didn't have a "diagnosable disease," that he "seemed well-adjusted." Finally, Spencer, a tad exasperated, told the doctor, "You are telling me everything that was *not* wrong with him."

Dr. Michael Brannon had a plausible hypothesis concerning Charlie's undiagnosable disease.

"Personality disorders are not a disease," the psychologist stated. "They are not diagnosed like schizophrenia, for instance. Personality disorders are a certain set of behaviors that go with that personality trait."

When his son was finally released, Herbert Brandt sold the family home in Fort Wayne, Indiana, and relocated with his entire family to Ormond Beach, Florida, to the same small house where they used to vacation, and where they had been only twenty-four hours before the incident. They never spoke of that incident again. Apparently Herbert, influenced by his rigid training as a youth under the Third Reich, did not believe in airing the family's secrets in public, while Angela did her father's bidding, and Jessica and Melanie were too little to remember anything. In time, it seemed they simply compartmentalized it.

Herbert remarried, and left again for Indiana with his new wife and two younger daughters. Angela and Charlie were left behind, and their grandparents came over from Germany to look after young Charlie, who was sixteen at the time. Angela was eighteen. Again, did Charlie experience fear of abandonment, as he had when he'd asked his sister not to leave him after the murder of his mother, the attack on his father, and the attempted assault on Angela herself?

According to the Fort Wayne *Gazette Journal's* Ron Shawgo, his father described Charlie as a quiet, shy kid. Everyone knew Charlie was unhappy when he moved from Connecticut, where he had grown up, to Indiana. His sister Angela said Charlie was overweight and was picked on by his peers. Charlie admittedly disliked school very much.

But he made a few friends while attending public school in Daytona Beach—especially his sister's boyfriend, Jim Graves. Seabreeze High School is a school of mostly surfers and jocks, yet Charlie collected stamps and played chess. He was never a discipline problem and made good grades. He was rather passive, his dad said. Charlie told his father that if he ever joined the military he'd be a medic, because he didn't believe in violence. Other, more popular kids would call someone like Charlie a nerd; he was so non-violent, his buddy Jim said, that he would rather pick up a bug and throw it outside than kill it.

However, at Seabreeze, Charlie seemed to blossom somewhat. Jim remembers Charlie was a year behind him. "I only saw him after class, like when he came over to see Angie and me, and when we went fishing. He had girlfriends in high school, had two that I remember. He seemed just like everybody else. It wasn't until I went on that vacation on the Keys when he went on about the heart that I thought, 'That was weird,' especially knowing what I knew."

Jim was obviously remembering the time on Charlie's boat, when, two days after his birthday, his wife Angie, Charlie's sister, left him, and he was berating her in very deprecating, derogatory terms. "I wanted to break her heart like she broke mine and I told Charlie." But Jim was not prepared for Charlie's recipe for revenge: "The best revenge is when you cut someone's heart out and eat it."

Jim said he wouldn't have thought anything of it; he would have thought the statement was one typical of young studs talking at a bar about killing a rival football team. However, Jim already knew what he knew. And he still had a week left with Charlie in the Keys. After all, the vacation away from heartbreak was fashioned for him, for Jim, by Charlie.

"After that came out of his mouth. I slept with one eye open. That was the first time around him that I felt trepidation and fear. And I couldn't talk to my friends about it, because nobody knew what I knew, and they would have laughed at me. And I was still brainwashed by the family's statements and by the psychiatrists' evaluations, and even by my family's statements that he deserved another chance."

Jim remembered that Charlie had done coke, after the bounty he found in Andros Island. "And he did dabble in psychedelic drugs, like LSD."

As to how Charlie had learned to make the precision cuts with which he dismembered some of his victims, the answer did not only lie in his proficiency with fishing, although that is a minor clue. "Charlie was already fishing when I met him," Jim said. "And he liked to cut the fish open while they were alive. We just figured he liked his fish freshly bled." That is not normal for most seasoned fishermen.

Kevin Shore, who went to the same high school as Charlie, lived with Charlie for a good bit in the early 1970's, fished with him, and went out on the town with him.

Kevin Shore first stated, "I don't really have much to say about Charlie, because it's all good things." Charlie's friends all seemed to think of him as "a good ol boy." But Kevin claimed Charlie was very smart. He had that "German intellect," he said, also mentioning that Charlie was not into any sports other than fishing.

And when the two friends went shark fishing, Kevin said, "Charlie would always gut and/or want me to gut the shark immediately. Charlie said, 'Hey man, there might be a foot or a leg or an arm in there.'" After Charlie's bloody crimes and dismemberments, Kevin now says he finds some significance in that sort of curiosity. It is not the curiosity of an avid sports fisherman, to be sure.

Kevin remembered they used to go down to Ponce Inlet where the boats would come in. Ponce Inlet is at the southernmost point of Daytona Beach and past Daytona Beach Shores, and is a town unto itself. It has several marinas and its residents pride themselves on their boats and on the quality of their catch.

The fishermen used to take bonito fish, and use the back-strap piece of them as bait. Bonito are very bloody fish, and Charlie either bought some of this bait off the fishermen, or procure his own. But in the freezer at the house Kevin and Charlie shared, Charlie stored large ice cubes, almost like ice blocks, made out of bonito blood. It was frozen blood cubes from the bonito fish. Either this was Charlie's clever way of preserving some valuable chum, or bait to attract fish, or perhaps the ice cubes contained something else. It is not too much of a stretch, considering Charlie's deviancy. In any case, it was an original strategy on his part, one way or another.

Donald Withers also said that Charlie was a great fisherman. The fishing buddies used to pay kids fifty cents to paddle their surfboards out into the ocean to throw their bloody bonito fish and blood ice blocks and buckets of meat blood which Charlie would get from restaurants, into the water so they could catch all sorts of sharks: blacktip, bull, and lemon sharks ranging between six and ten feet.

Kevin remembers that after Charlie found the coke in the Keys, "He came back home, got connected with the buyer, and drove to Miami and sold the stash." He stayed in Miami for a while. "When Charlie got back from Miami," his friend remembered, "he was broad-shouldered, had a shaved chest, was drinking vodka straight from the bottle, and was completely blown out on coke. I had seen Charlie drink before, but nothing like this." The image is sort of chilling, like something out of *"Natural Born Killers"* or *"Apocalypse Now."*

Kevin explained how much easier times were back then: "The partying, the drugging, getting away with it all."

Kevin and Charlie and Jim were all friends, and had gone to high school together; and one day, Kevin said, Jim unloaded the "secret" he had been withholding for all those years—the secret about Charlie's past.

About two or three days later, Kevin was parked in the Publix parking lot in Daytona Beach Shores, reading the paper, and came across an article about Charlie's final crimes that he had just committed in Orlando.

Kevin immediately called Jim and shouted over the telephone: "Jim, you need to go read the paper right now!" Jim replied, confusedly, "Why? What?" Kevin repeated: "You just need to go read the paper right now! Look at Section Three!"

When asked about the possibility that, given his age—Kevin was eighteen and Charlie was twenty back when they hung out together—and the time frame, Charlie could have been killing then, Kevin's immediate response was, "Sure!" The friend was prepared to back that up with the narration of an interesting, yet somewhat terrifying story.

"Charlie used to come home from working at Bahama Joe's, the seafood joint, in the kitchen," the then-roommate began. "And when he came home at night, he smelled absolutely awful. He was wearing his work outfit, but also those big awkward rubber boots you wear to either fly-fish or trudge through deep water. And all over his boots and his clothes would be blood." Kevin stated that Charlie claimed it was the kitchen that smelled so awful, and that the blood all over him was because the "meat was really fresh."

Folks who are kitchen workers, especially in seafood places, do not come home covered in blood, nor could the few who were interviewed for this passage explain why someone would, let alone have to, wear rubber boots on the job.

For all of this, there might have been plausible explanations. But had Charlie been alive, there would have been plenty of circumstantial evidence in his case, aside from all the direct evidence of the bodies. Investigators have found significant evidence that Charlie was a student of his "craft."

Special Agent D'Ambrosia points to an anatomy chart investigators found in Charlie's house on Big Pine Key. She explains the most relevent connection with this disturbing poster, which was of the body of a woman with her hair in a bun on top of her head, one half depicting muscle tissue and the other the skeleton and bones:

"He had a sexual obsession with body parts, organs, necrophilia, peeping, women's lingerie, etc. He enjoyed viewing a variety of sexually deviant Internet sites and received *Victoria's Secret* catalogues." Investigators found a lot of necrophiliac sites on his computer, and the *Victoria's Secret* catalogues, all mailed to Charlie, were stashed in his attic. The necrophiliac sites are very graphic.

An analysis of Charlie's computer, seized from his home in Big Pine Key, revealed that he regularly visited several Internet sites with topics like "erotic horror" and "death-fetish erotica" and "drop-dead gorgeous." When forensic computer analysts reviewed Charlie's computer, they found he frequented sites depicting nude women in violent and bloody scenes, or who were made to look dead or injured.

"All these things fueled his fantasies and his particular desires," profiler D'Ambrosia said. "I took the female anatomy chart to be just another item that he viewed to fuel his fantasy of dismemberment, et cetera. One must ask, why would he need a full chart affixed to the back of the bedroom door? If there was an interest or curiosity in anatomy by a person, do they actually post it on the back of their bedroom door? I would say no. It might be accessible in the office—and they had an office set up in the second bedroom—but not the bedroom."

In "*People of the Lie, The Hope for Healing Human Evil*," M. Scott Peck, M.D. references Erich Fromm's broadened definition of necrophilia "to include the desire of certain people to control others—to make them controllable, to foster their dependency...." and further defines the "necrophilic character type" as someone "whose aim is to avoid the inconvenience of life by transforming others into obedient automatons, robbing them of their humanity." That was what Jeffrey Dahmer did, taking it to the extreme. But nobody knows if Charlie engaged in cannibalism.

Dr. Michael Brannon has an opinion on the subject:

"We really believe, with such an odd and unusual behavior, that there is some biological disorder. In some places where cannibalism is accepted, that would be the norm. But in our society, where it is such a taboo, something must have happened in terms of a biological disorder. So yes, he may well have engaged in cannibalism. Body parts can become trophies. If no such trophies are found, they become cannibalized." Some of the body parts of the women that Charlie disemboweled were never found.

Marty Morgenrath, another one of Teri and Mary Lou's sisters, may hold some sort of explanation.

"My husband and I visited them, Charlie and Teri, in 2000." Marty is a post-traumatic therapist. "I gave a massage to my sister and offered to give one to Charlie, and he refused. But when we all went to the beach I noticed he had a large scar in his chest down to his abdomen. I think he'd had some physical trauma as a very young infant."

"Charlie was very quiet, very controlled, in his emotional responses, and we thought, something had happened to him when he was younger. It was some kind of abdominal surgery when he was an infant," Marty added. "I have spoken to other experts in trauma therapy," stated Teri's sister. "That kind of early surgical trauma could have some psychological repercussions."

Charlie kept the anatomy chart behind his bedroom door, the bedroom he shared with his wife. Did he need that stimulus to make love? Perhaps his desire was to have her be submissive. In the end, he finally got his wish with her, and with Michelle, with whom he was obsessed. Jeffrey Dahmer kept his victims' parts, fueled by the same desire, and also from a fear of abandonment. Dahmer had been left alone in his family home by his parents for one whole year. And both Ted Bundy and Gary Ridgway engaged in post-mortem sex with corpses as a means of control.

As to what Charlie did with the body parts that were not found, Special Agent D'Ambrosia is hesitant to speculate, and does it with a disclaimer:

"It is against everything I do to guess randomly without basis, which is what I would be doing if I guessed what he did with body parts. The best I can say is that given his fantasy-based behaviors/obsessions, it is possible that he would utilize souvenirs to relive his crimes for the purpose of sexual gratification. What would support this is the fact that there were body parts missing (e.g. taken to fantasize). If his intent was mere dissection/disarticulation, then he would not have taken the hearts (and in one case the head) of his victims. What would be the point? There are documented cases where other offenders who took body parts either consumed them or, in the cases with missing heads, buried them to unearth them later for the purpose of masturbation while fantasizing. There are cases where the offender stored parts in freezers in foil and/or plastic wrap. I also had another case involving the removal of a body part that was later used in a stew made by the offender, which he generously cooked for a group of people.

"With Charlie, it would be a guess to say if he buried the body parts if he consumed them, and I won't weigh in on that. All I can say is he did remove body parts, he was highly fantasy-oriented, so at a minimum you can deduce they were instruments of fantasy for sexual gratification. Logically there is no need to take something if you will not 'use' it sometime in the future. What can't be ignored is that with his last victim, he did not consume any organs or body parts, when he certainly had the opportunity to do so. Now, because he committed suicide and likely was planning the suicide in advance, he would have had no need to bury/store/preserve body parts if the intent was to later unearth them to relive his actions… he knew he wasn't going to be present in the future to do this."

And sure enough, Michelle's body parts were all left inside her room.

Jim Graves had one experience he found peculiar, when Charlie and Teri had recently married and Jim was single and playing music gigs in the Keys.

Jim was staying at Charlie and Teri's house.

"I was at the house and they had both gone to work. I was still young and a night owl, and hanging around in bars. During the day I was looking for something to read, and underneath the coffee table there was one of those very basic 'how to have good sex' books. Now, I can't help but wonder if he was deficient in that department. I was twenty-eight at the time and Charlie was twenty-seven, and I remember thinking to myself, he should know how to do it by now. I remember reading those books when I was seventeen!"

But again, before Teri, there was Carol Lynn Sullivan and Andros Island, and many other instances when, from the accounts of Teri's friends, Charlie would have been considered just a lecher with fantasies about extra-marital activities. These activities may be considered despicable, but do not account for a serial killer who disemboweled his victims. And they certainly do not account for someone who does not know anything about sex.

After all, on September 20, 1978, Carol Lynn Sullivan disappeared from a rural bus stop in Osteen, and two weeks later, her head was found stuffed in a rusty paint can in a remote spot near Deltona.

By then, Charlie had graduated from Seabreeze High School and had earned an Associate of Science degree from Daytona Beach Community College. He was working in nearby Flagler County. Her body was never recovered.

Special Agent D'Ambrosia offered her knowledge of a serial killer's "cooling-off period" as she viewed it in relation to Charlie.

"You cannot predict an individual's cooling-off period, because there is no set timeframe for such an event," explained the experienced profiler. "The term 'cooling-off period' was originally coined to describe/differentiate between the different types of killers: mass, spree, serial, et cetera. The definition for serial murder included an emotional cooling off period between events, whereas the spree murder had no emotional cooling-off; it was a continuous event, even if it occurred over an extended period of time. We do often look at what was going on during a cooling-off period especially if you have a sexually fantasy-motivated crime. Those urges/ desires just don't stop. But also, they don't necessarily constantly exist on a fixed schedule. So they occur when they occur. What we have seen is that a cooling-off period can occur or be extended when an offender is engaged in behaviors that tend to satisfy the urges. Having said that, not every single serial killer with a cooling-off period has to satiate his urges to keep from committing the next crime. The next crime may have occurred because of a precipitating stressor prior to the crime. So, back to Charlie: he was satisfying urges/fantasies by engaging in other behaviors that may have satisfied his fantasy needs, such as the Internet searches that provided information/interaction regarding necrophilia."

D'Ambrosia, however, had not been apprised either of Carol Lynn Sullivan's murder, nor of Charlie's stint in Andros Island.

Carol Lynn Sullivan may have been Charlie's first killing, Jim now shudders to think.

"I thought he had done it from that time at the dinner table," he recalled. Charlie's reaction when both young men were having dinner at Jim's mother's house and Mrs. Graves mentioned that a young girl's head was found inside a paint can.

"I have a perfect picture in my mind of what he looked like when he started laughing. He looked evil! It gave me chills. I thought, what's funny about this? I had a gut feeling he did it. He literally had a mouthful of food and spit it out, laughing."

Up until then, Charlie had been under the watchful eyes of his sister, his father, and his friend Jim. Then, he was staying at Jim's mother's house while he attended Daytona Beach Community College; his father had moved away, and Jim was also away at school. "There was nobody around him who knew," Jim pointed out.

But Jim, who had gone to high school with Charlie, and was married to his sister Angela, holds a theory in opposition to the cooling-off period hypothesis.

"One unexplored avenue was Andros Island," he stated. "And if that happened, those poor mothers deserve to know what happened to their daughters." Jim doesn't believe they will, though. He does believe "Charlie was killing over there. He was there when he was twenty-two and he was there for seven years. When I was talking to the FDLE they told me they were looking for every place he had been, and looked for MOs. I said, 'What about the Bahamas?' I thought that might have something to do with why he was drinking so much then. It was funny, because they were running a drug interdiction operation and getting high on coke. All he had to do was go to town, get drunk, and get a black girl," Jim stated in a disparaging tone about crimes he believes have not been solved.

"And Charlie was a racist!" He would have been working in the Bahamas after Carol Lynn Sullivan's head was found," he added, implying Charlie would have thought nothing at all about taking and raping a black woman.

The scuttlebutt—mostly in Fort Wayne spread by the media whenever the murder of his mother was mentioned—was that Charlie's first trigger had been the accidental shooting of his pet dog over the Christmas vacation by his father. It was not true. Charlie himself said he was going to cry, but did not, and spent the next two hours hunting with his dad. And Herbert stated that after he had shot at the woods to get the dog out and accidentally shot him, Charlie hadn't reacted at all, and this really concerned him.

When the police questioned Charlie about his motivation for the murder of his mother and shooting of his father, he answered that he did not really know why he had done it.

"A combination of things," he said. "A lot of work, tests to make up. I had to make up my interim card. Everything sort of snapped in my mind. I felt like I never felt before."

Charlie was born in Connecticut in 1956. It was where the family relocated after immigrating to Texas. It was where Charlie grew up, went to school, and made friends.

Herbert Brandt was transferred to Fort Wayne, to the Harvester plant in 1968.

Charlie felt he did not fit in, and did not make friends. He did not like it in Fort Wayne, Indiana.

And he said he did not remember how many shots he'd fired at his parents that night of January 3, 1971.

"After the first shot, I can't remember how many shots. I think the gun was empty."

It was his older sister, Angela, the hippie fifteen-year-old who had Beatles posters on her bedroom walls, who had persuaded him to stop, after her brother tried to shoot her and began strangling her.

"We'll run away to a hippie commune," Angie said to appease him and to erase the glazed, manic look in his eyes, a look that had really frightened her. "I won't leave you, I promise." Again, Angela, had known her little brother was trying to ease his sense of abandonment. Why?

Police officers had driven Charlie to the Allen County Jail. After a few days, one officer took him to the hospital to see his ailing father. Charlie asked for permission to cry. Was it on account of Herbert's strict upbringing, or Charlie's inner programming, that he felt to present an appropriate façade to the world?

At the hospital, Charlie apologized to his father. Herbert told him that everything would be all right, and the family never spoke about the incident again—except the time when Charlie told Angela he was going to get married to Teri Helfrich. Then Angela, who was thirty at the time, insisted her brother tell Teri the truth about his past.

"Yes, tell Teri everything," she said. "If you do, and she doesn't marry you, then you'll just have to live with that. If you don't, somehow, sometime, she might find out, and that's not going to go over well."

Charlie acquiesced and told her sister he would take her advice.

Charlie and Teri were married August 29, 1986. No family members on either side were invited.

And nobody could tell with any degree of certainty whether Teri Helfrich, now Brandt, knew the truth about her husband's past. "She would not have married him if she had known," her sister and Michelle's mother Mary Lou insisted. Bill Jones, Michelle's father and Teri's brother-in-law, believes he has a logical answer. "Teri never could keep a secret," he said. "Sooner or later she would have blurted it out."

Charlie's sister Angela was not so certain, either, even though Charlie had assured her that he would tell Teri.

However, according to some witnesses, when Angela welcomed Teri to the family, she called her new sister-in-law a special person, saying, "Charlie told you about himself, and you married him anyway? You must really love him."

Teri hugged Angela and smiled in acknowledgement, Angela thought, and said to herself, "Good. She knows and she accepts him."

Charlie and Teri moved to their own home in Big Pine Key early in 1989, after renting for a while. In July 1989, just a few months later, a fisherman found the body of Sherry Perisho floating, facedown, under the Big Pine Key Bridge, approximately a thousand feet from Charlie and Teri's home.

Mary Lou Jones recalled that their mother had always encouraged them to keep a diary. Teri kept a daily planner where she wrote mostly about mundane daily occurrences, such as "Good day!" or "A good dinner." That began to change in 1993, when the "good day" became "weird," or when "Charlie was away for the whole weekend."

The Florida Department of Law Enforcement provided the planner, with locations for Charlie Brandt. Teri's sister, Mary Lou, and Teri's best friend on Big Pine Key, Melanie Fecher, supplied additional information:

"Teri and I always talked about not wanting children," Melanie said. "That must be what she meant."

However, Teri's daily planner seems to speak from beyond the grave.

On Tuesday, October 5, 2004, Detective Sergeant Patricia Dally provided Special Agents D'Ambrosia and Edward Royal with a timeline, which Sergeant Dally had created from various entries in Teri's diaries, dated from 1985 through 2003. The entries noted by Dally include dates on which Charlie traveled to other cities, states, and countries. Dally also incorporated in the timeline, the dates of three unsolved homicides in Monroe County.

The following is the timeline prepared by Sergeant Dally:

CHARLIE TERI LOCATION OR COMMENT

1985 April 17—blind date with Charlie
April 25— first*
18-Jul 21—Nassau, Bahamas
August 5—Charlie asked me to move in with him.
September 4—first night in apartment
18-Oct 20-Oct—St.Augustine, FL
Nov. 7 17-Nov—Nassau, Bahamas
1986 18 Jan—Melbourne, FL
Feb 26—Charlie's Dad, Gail, Melody talked
20-Mar 23-Mar—Key Largo, FL then home Ormond Beach, FL
2-May 5-May—Fly to New Orleans, LA
Charlie asked me to marry him
11-Jul 18-Jul—St. Lucia, Bahamas
July 26—new apartment
29-Aug 2-Sep—Islamorada, FL wedding day
Sept. 12—Charlie interview in Key West

Sept. 26 29-Sep—Washington, DC

10-Oct 13-Oct—the Keys, FL

October 22—New home (rent) the keys

Dec. 9—bought boat

1987 22 -May 25-May—Daytona, FL

June 10th—weird feeling

29-Aug 3-Sep—Miami, FL to Cozumel, Mexico

13-Dec—LA

24-Dec 27-Dec—Orlando, FL

1988 24-Jan 5-Feb—Charlie leaves for the Cape

29-Jan 31-Jan—Teri-Melbourne then at the Cape

March 18—Weird day

23-Mar Mach 28—Phoenix, AZ

26-May 30-May—Ormond Beach, FL

July 2—Patricia Lorenza Homicide

3-Jul 15-Jul—Washington, DC Norfolk to home

August 25—weird day

October 8—house hunting

20-Oct 23-Oct—Dallas,TX

December 9—closed on house Ranger Ave, Big Pine Key, FL

December 16—Lisa Sanders Homicide

27-Dec 30-Dec—Daytona, FL

1989 18-Feb 19 - Feb—Boat Show then to the Everglades, FL

27-Apr 7-May—New Orleans, LA

May 8—weird day

7-Jun 10-Jun—Ft. Lauderdale, FL

July 11—rough conversation

July 19—Sherry Perisho Homicide

28-Sep 2-Oct—Jackson bound - [For the wedding of Teri's friend, Melanie Fecher.]

22-Nov Nov 25—Melbourne, FL

1990 17-Jan 20-Jan—Miss [with the Fechers]

21-Jan 28-Jan—Hawaii

15-Mar 17-Mar—West Palm Beach,FL

26-Apr 1-May—Ft. Walton Beach, FL

1-May 2-May—Orlando, FL

6-Jul 9-Jul—Homestead, Vanderbilt Bch, Sanibel, FL

12-Oct 16-Oct—Boston, MA

22-Dec 24-Dec—Ormond Beach and Orlando, FL

1991 February 14—Valentine Homicide

May 2—[Teri stops writing in planner and starts another planner.]

5-Jun 6-Jun—Miami, FL

5-Jul 12-Jul—Colorado

July 22—Charlie got no contract news

August 13—weird day, rough, runaway and hide feeling

5-Oct 10-Oct—St. Pete and Sanibel, FL

30-Oct 3-Nov—Orlando, FL

24-Dec 28-Dec—Orlando, FL

1992 Jan 12—Charlie on meds

Jan 17—Charlie lost contract

18-Jan 19-Jan—Everglades/Fl City, FL

Jan 22—Charlie gone at 3:30AM

May 27—Charlie fired

8-Jun 14-Jun—Maryland

11-Jul 17-Jul—Denver and Keystone, Colorado [Teri went on staff retreat with the dentist she was working with, and the staff.]

July 13—Charlie starts meds

14-Oct 18-Oct—Bahamas

Nov. 25—Teri turned into a witch/Charlie hurt

Dec 14—Charlie's family

1993 Feb 2—start meds

March 5—Deb Harrison [mental health Ph.D.]

14-Apr 18-Apr—homestead to Sanibel, FL

July 15—Charlie a little depressed

18-Jul 26-Jul—[Teri's father has a stroke and passes away]

24-Jul 26-Jul—[Charlie arrives Orlando]

26-Jul 5-Aug—South Carolina-Funeral [Charlie leaves 30th?]

Aug 22—walked to the site for lunch

Aug 30—Melanie called hurting bad

Sept. 16—started to talk things out-talkative time a bit emotional

Oct. 27—a bit impatient with Charlie

30-Oct 2-Dec—Miami, Tampa, Panama City, to FWB [Teri stays with her mother after her father's death.]

Nov 5—Charlie left message did not talk

Nov. 6—Charlie called very emotional

Nov. 11—Charlie called a bit upset

Nov. 24—Charlie called real emotional

20-Dec 21-Dec—Orlando, FL

1994 Jan 17—Charlie had a rough day

1-Mar 4-Mar—Bahamas

31-May—Miami, FL

29-Jun 6-Jul—Cormel, Point Sur, California [Teri reunion with her sisters for her mother's birthday, she turned 70.]

Aug 11— weird day

18-Oct 20-Oct—Stuart, FL

Oct 24—problem solving

Nov 24—weird day

14-Dec—Miami, FL

Dec. 24—Upsetting night [in 1995 book]

1995 11-May 16-May—Ft. Walton Beach, FL

July 5—sad day

July 21—weird talk and not a good night

20-Sep 3-Oct—Spokane WA and California

Dec. 25—weird evening

1996 9-Jan 12-Jan—Daytona, FL

31-Jan 10-Feb—Ft. Walton Beach, FL [Teri and her sister Pat arrive to help her ill mother.]

18-Mar 21-Mar—Homestead and Coral Gables, FL

*6-May 16-May —PA and Maryland [Teri and her sisters help mother
move to Maryland - funeral services for mother.]*

19-Sep 2-Oct—Hawaii

1997 Jan 1—emotional

9-Sep 17-Sep—California [Teri visits her sister Marty]

26-Oct 31-Oct—Melbourne, FL

7-Nov—Orlando, FL

1998 17-Mar 23-Mar—St. Johns Bahamas

26-Aug 30-Aug—Daytona, FL

23-Sep 28-Sep—Orlando, FL

Oct 8—lost it

22-Dec 29-Dec—Maryland

1999 Jan 29—Charlie played with computer

4-May 10-May—Bahamas

16-Sep 26-Sep—California

2000 31-May 3—Jun - Sanibel, FL

June 21—weird feeling

2001 27-Feb—Miami, FL (Dr. Chase)

21-Mar 23-Mar—Daytona, FL

15-May 24-May—California

July 12—Dr. Pruett

9-Aug 10-Aug—Fl. City, FL

*2002 14-Jan 17-Jan—NC [Teri and Charlie went to see Teri's parents and
bought a car]*

14-May 21-May—DC

18-Jun—Miami, FL

4-Jul—Orlando, FL

12-Nov 21-Nov—Melbourne, FL

2003 15-May 20-May—NC [Teri went to a sisters reunion]

14-Apr 16-Apr—Melbourne, FL

15-May 20-May—Orlando to NC
8-Jul 11-Jul—Melbourne, FL
13-Jul 19-Jul —Melbourne, FL [the trips to Melbourne were to see Melanie
Fecher, who had moved.]
20-Jul 27-Jul—Las Vegas, Reno, Lake Tahoe
26-Nov—Orlando, FL

Some of Teri's and Michelle's friends can account for some of these times, and states of mind.

Suzy Hamilton, for instance, who had a thirty-million-dollar account with Michelle at The Golf Channel, remembered something out-of-the-ordinary that happened when both women were very young.

"Michelle had become one of my best friends in the world," said the client, who'd loved her new account, and its rep. "I met both Charlie and Teri and at the time I didn't think much of him, but Michelle and I went on trips a lot; to Key West, for instance. On one of those occasions, Teri and Charlie came to meet me and I had some business friends with me, and we all had our boyfriends and other friends with us. In short, we were a large group." Hamilton prefaced what later occurred. "We went out to dinner, all of us, including Charlie and Teri. We later went to the pier to see the boats. And then we realized we'd lost one of our friends; she kind of disappeared on us! The next morning we couldn't find her. It was noon the next day when she finally resurfaced. And she said, 'I don't know what happened; I don't remember anything!' It turned out she woke up in the bathroom in the middle of the night. She had been sitting next to Charlie all night, and Charlie had offered himself as the designated driver. I don't know if any of that is of any significance."

It may not be. Both Teri's and Michelle's friends now see a lot of things in hindsight.

As for Charlie choosing to be the designated driver, profiler D'Ambrosia has an easy explanation.

D'Ambrosia met Teri's sisters on Big Pine Key and asked them about Charlie's alleged solicitous attitude towards his wife, as witnessed and recounted by everyone who knew the couple.

"It sounds like it fits Teri's sisters' description of Charlie always being the 'caretaker,' for lack of a better description, whenever there was a group together socializing. Everyone insisted that he was a social person and a nice guy when the case first broke. I proclaimed that this would change with time, when everyone truly understood his behavior, or when they began to dissect how he really behaved.

"I asked her sisters when I bumped into them in the Keys, if he had ever actually sat and engaged in conversation with them, because as they described him back then, was he was always 'doting' on Teri and them in social settings. He would get them drinks and jump up and refill them when they got low, he would prepare snacks, et cetera. Basically, he served as the waitstaff.

"When I asked if he'd ever actually participated in the social gatherings and preferred that—instead, perhaps he was serving everyone because he was uncomfortable with sitting with them in the social setting—this is when I got the 'aha!' moment. I told them that perhaps it was his way of avoiding actual social interaction and conversations. On the surface he was Mr. Nice Guy, the Host with the Most, but in actuality I believe he was avoiding prolonged social interaction. His offering to be the DD served this purpose, and put him in close proximity to the other girls. We understood that Charlie was a little bored, unhappy with the marriage and/or Teri. He wasn't perhaps as attracted to her anymore. His hitting on the other girls is not so much weird, as it is an indication that he was a common lech looking for extramarital activities."

As for the young woman, Suzy's friend, "disappearing" after sitting next to Charlie all night, there might be an equally mundane explanation. Everyone in the group was drinking a lot; it's what young people do in the Keys. Perhaps the young woman had simply had too much, ran to the bathroom, and there, passed out. One thing is certain: If Charlie Brandt, serial killer and stalker of women, had had any designs on Suzy's friend, she would not have resurfaced at noon the next day—perhaps not ever.

Now, maybe this scenario holds the truth, and maybe it is coincidental, but Jim noticed that Charlie and Teri's behavior towards him began to change after they were married for a while. This is not surprising, considering the upheaval that was going on in the Big Pine Key home, behind closed doors, between the couple, according to entries in Teri's planner.

"They started acting like they were the adults and I wasn't grown up because I was single," Jim said, with a sense of surprise still. "I attributed it to both of them back then, but in retrospect, Teri was very fun-loving, and I think it was Charlie. I think he wanted me away from her. Now I think he probably committed a lot of atrocities in the Bahamas. It wasn't till he left the islands that he wanted to meet a girl." And then, maybe, Charlie was trying to isolate her.

But if Jim was puzzled at finding a basic "how-to" book on having sex under Charlie and Teri's coffee table, investigators were even more puzzled when they found a female anatomy chart hung beside their bedroom door.

"I was told the chart was Charlie's, by investigators," said profiler D'Ambrosia. "If that was true, and it was not Teri's, then I would view that as being consistent with his fantasies and paraphilic desires. He had a sexual obsession with body parts, organs, necrophilia, peeping, women's lingerie, et cetera. He enjoyed viewing a variety of sexually deviant Internet sites and received *Victoria's Secret* catalogues. All of these fueled his fantasies and his particular desires."

Forensic computer experts found that Charlie visited all sorts of websites about necrophilia, and he did receive *Victoria's Secret* catalogues, which he stashed carefully away. He did refer to Michelle as his "Victoria's Secret." And as D'Ambrosia pointed out: "The anatomy chart isn't paired with a specific event, but could provide that same sexual excitement as a trophy or souvenir."

If the anatomy chart was behind their bedroom door, Charlie had to see it whenever he and Teri made love. It is a gruesome thought when viewed in conjunction with the sexual act on a marital bed, but perhaps for Charlie it was better than the sex book Jim had spotted under the coffee table.

D'Ambrosia reconstructed Charlie's crimes, and drew some conclusions based on the injuries from the murders inside the home of Michelle Jones.

"He killed Teri first," D'Ambrosia stated. "It looked like Teri was on the sofa and she had been drinking—wine, I believe. She may have dozed off on the sofa. All of them had been drinking that day. As I remember, it looked like Michelle had gone to take a shower, and he blitzed her or surprised her there."

Michelle:
- *Was found nude on the bed with head removed and positioned to the side of the body "overlooking" the body (as though observing the process of disarticulation-removal of body parts). Did he want her to "see his work?"*
- *Chest cut open*
- *Heart removed and lying beside body*
- *Left leg removed—on bed*
- *Both breasts removed—on bed*
- *Left arm partially severed—no[t] completely removed*
- *Liver, some intestines, abdominal wall removed and put inside lined garbage can next to foot of bed*
- *Removed parts, especially head, devoid of blood (looked like he cleaned her face and smoothed her hair) [This is what profilers call "undoing,"*

trying to make it seem as though the murder didn't occur.]

- *Blood noted as finger-marks on limbs (probably from his holding them to slice/cut)*
- *Bed not much blood due to post-mortem removal*
- *Cause of death was a single stab wound to the chest. This sharp force injury was ante-mortem [before death] and severed the mid sternum, slightly up to down and centered. Cut through pericardium and right ventricle, and severed the aorta. (Deep single stab wound that caused death)*
- *There were contusions on her right hand and thumb and right foot and leg. There was also a superficial abrasion to the right hand. Bruising indicates the injury happened before death [due to circulation]. It is unknown if this is considered "defensive." There are none of the typical defensive wounds we see in stabbing deaths: cuts and gashes to the hands. [This would indicate being struck or striking someone, but given their days-long "partying" state, it's just as likely she fell getting out of the hot tub.]*
- *There are blood clots in the lungs (hemothorax) indicating the chest injuries etc. resulting in the filling of blood in the lungs before (or while) dying.*
- *The stab wound would have been immediately incapacitating.*
- *There is a blood-stained blue tank top with a "vertical cut" on the shirt below the neckline, in the sink basin. So she was killed while wearing her shirt. The rest was post mortem and done on the bed. (ergo: why I thought she was blitzed in the bathroom) I suppose it's possible she ran from him there, but there are no signs of struggle. There are perfume bottles, etc. on the counter, her jeans skirt is on the counter, cell phone, moisturizer, etc. Perhaps getting ready to get in the shower?*
- *Her panties and bra are in the bedroom on the floor with other items: bloodstained pink panties cut/torn, blue bloodstained panties intact with a maxi pad attached, bloodstained pink bra cut/torn, section of a bloodstained pink bra cut/torn away, bloodstained pair of torn orange*

panties, bloodstained orange bra intact, 4 bloodstained towels (hand, bath that match, 2 beach towels) I think were used to clean up the blood on the body parts to make it look the way he wanted. Also the detectives said the cuts/tears were on one side of the panties.

- *There was a pair of Champion gym shorts (tag removed) and an American Outdoors t-shirt (tag removed) on the floor with the lingerie/panties, also bloodstained. In the bedroom with all of Teri and Charlie's belongings were suitcases containing clothing that had all the clothing tags cut out. So these were Charlie's clothes on the floor with her panties, etc. He changed. I think it's likely he removed his clothing and put on Michelle's panties (why he cut the one side) Since we already know Charlie was a paraphile [engaged in sexually deviant behavior such as necrophilia and peeping] we know that Charlie would likely have engaged in other behaviors regarded as sexually deviant, paraphilic behavior because research shows that paraphilic behavior is clustered. Meaning research has shown that if there is evidence of a person engaging in one sexually deviant behavior, the likelihood is high they will engage in others. Cross-dressing (transvestitism) would not be a stretch here. So perhaps Charlie was also cross-dressing with the undergarment of his victim. Except if Charlie did it, it was only this one time, with Michelle's "Victoria's Secret" underwear.*

Teri:

- *Wearing only a t-shirt. Her pajama bottoms were removed/pulled all the way down.—Why? To humiliate and degrade her?*
- *She has multiple stab wounds to the chest. There were 10 stab wounds noted in the mid and lower chest area. The 11th stab wound was actually an "exit" stab wound in the back associated with a lower chest stab wound that was over 18 cm in depth (wow, that's deep) and exited her back. This damaged many vital organs inside.*

- *She had defensive wounds on her left hand. Perhaps she awoke? (when she approached her?!) or was just very inebriated when he approached. She was dressed for bed, on the sofa, and had a glass of wine on the table. She could have dozed off.*
- *Her t-shirt had numerous cuts to the front that corresponded with the sharp-force injuries to the torso.*
- *Her pants were pulled down—this is both voyeuristic and degrading.*

Charlie:
- *Only injury was the ligature mark*
- *He was clothed hanging in the garage, there was a steak knife on the hood of the car below him but he hadn't stabbed himself*
- *He had obviously changed clothes before hanging. His other bloody clothes were in Michelle's room.*
- *He knew he what he was going to do. He had visited his dad (one day or two days before) in Melbourne while they were staying with Michelle. Essentially he said goodbye to dad. He told dad he loved him, etc. He'd never done this before; they didn't have that kind of relationship where they told each other this (so I was told)*

After the September 2004 deaths of Charlie and Teri Brandt and Michelle Jones, their families issued a brief statement through the sheriff's office. It reads: "Like everyone, we struggle to understand why."

Police will probably never know how many people Charlie killed in his lifetime.

But Special Agent D'Ambrosia believes there was a precipitating stressor to the final murders, and to Charlie's suicide.

"I believe Charlie was faced with a precipitating stressor before the murder of Michelle," said the profiler. "Charlie's employer was in the process of either selling the company or being absorbed into another corporation. In other words, there was a major change in employment management. As a result the employees were required to undergo a background investigation. Charlie had worked for this company for a long time and had not had to face the prospect of people learning about his murdering and attempting to murder his family in Indiana. This would have likely come out in the background—or at least he was likely concerned with the prospect of this coming out. He worked for a radar installation company and security was a major issue, especially in a post-911 world. Adding to his likely concern and/or paranoia on this issue was the fact that he had wanted to be a pilot in his younger years, and when he submitted his licensing application and indicated (or the background determined, I don't know which) he had been a murderer, he was not licensed. So he already had an experience of not attaining a cherished goal because of his background. From what we could determine, he was concerned about the background, and about his employer learning of his past. He would have lost the great career he'd established."

From the crime scene reconstruction, D'Ambrosia describes a perverse possible scenario as well:

"It is entirely possible that Charlie had worn Michelle's panties. I deduced this from the scene details. Her lacy panties were removed from her dresser opposite the bed in which she was lying dismembered. Those panties were on the floor in the midst of the trash can containing her organs, et cetera. If the scene is reconstructed, the panties were put there after the murder, and they were all cut on one side. So, we thought logically, why would someone cut away one side? There is no overtly functional reason for her to have done that. But a reason could be that someone cut the side so that they could pull them up on themselves. So there is the possibility that he wore them, or tried to. This is not a leap in behavior for him. Since he was engaging in dismemberment and had necrophilia fantasies, he obviously was engaging in paraphilic behavior. Research has proven that if you determine an individual has engaged in one form of sexually deviant behavior, the likelihood is that they are engaging in between three and ten sexually deviant behaviors. This is why it is said that paraphilic behavior is clustered. They engage in more than one behavior. So to dress in women's clothing is completely plausible in his case."

Also, both employers and authorities would have known about his not only botching the drug interdiction operation, but turning it into a drug-dealing business, and taking the drugs himself. Who knows if they might have found out about Andros Island?

There is, of course, again, the shocking case of Russell Williams, a colonel of the Canadian forces who, as a star pilot, flew Queen Elizabeth on several occasions. Williams, unbeknownst to his neighbors in Tweed, Canada, who referred to the stalker as "the Tweed Creeper," was convicted of creeping into female neighbors' homes, taking their underwear, and shooting his own photo wearing them. He then escalated to murder and was convicted and sentenced to two life sentences.

It is still shocking to see the photos of Williams, which he carefully preserved and saved, wearing women's underwear.

D'Ambrosia and Sergeant Dennis Haley were dispatched on hurricane detail in 2004, the summer of the three deadly storms. As they were told the details of the Jones/Brandt murders, Haley said they looked at each other and had an "aha!" moment when they both said: "That's the guy who killed Perisho!" They had been trying to solve the Sherry Perisho murder, a cold case by now, since she had been found floating on the water under the Big Pine Key Bridge in 1989.

After the September 2004 slayings of Teri Brandt and her niece, the Seminole County Sheriff's office sent out an international bulletin to other agencies around the country and the world, to find out if there were any matching crimes.

"We knew right away it wasn't the first time he'd done this," Seminole County Sheriff Donald Eslinger said.

Charlie's travel placed him in Germany and Holland at the time some similar crimes were committed there. But no concrete evidence came back. And no concrete evidence was found in the Carol Lynn Sullivan case. In Andros Island, nobody looked for any evidence.

"And, of course, nothing is just that simple in behavior," noted D'Ambrosia. "I find there are coexisting motivations/reasons for most everything. Add to the above: Charlie and his wife had evacuated the Keys because of hurricanes twice that season. Both times they relocated to Michelle's house. It was determined in the investigation that Charlie had a 'thing' for Michelle. So he is obsessed, as someone said, with her and now he has to be in her presence for an extended period of time. (The 'carrot' dangling before him perhaps—the object of his affection and his obsession.) Putting all these stressors together for Charlie likely created a serial killer perfect storm." And yes, Charlie and Teri had been at Michelle's house for a week in 2000, before she bought her home, when she lived in a sprawling two bedroom apartment.

What follows is an interview with Detective Rob Hemmert, of the Seminole County Sheriff's Department, dated September 21, 2004.

Ernest "Skip" Taylor is an electronics technician who has worked the "Fat Albert" Blimp since 1992 with Charlie. Skip and his ex-wife had met Charlie and Teri a couple of years prior to the murders, met playing volleyball out on the ball field on Big Pine Key. Skip Taylor described their relationship as "very good friends," and when Hemmert asked him what kind of a guy Charlie had been, Skip's response was not unlike the consensus about good friend Charlie and good neighbor Charlie and good husband Charlie.

"The only fault Charlie had was that he had no faults. Just a nice guy," his friend Skip said. "All-around sweetheart of a guy. When you got into work he was always pleasant, always, 'Hi Skip, how ya doing?' I don't know, just a really nice guy."

He hadn't been as close friends with Teri, he clarified when prompted by the detective.

And then Hemmert, who had taken his time, got to the question:

"Did he ever talk about Teri's family at all?" the detective asked for an opener. And there was the obsession: "Yeah, he talked about the niece and the sisters; although I had met the sisters at a social function a few years back, I didn't really know them, and I never met the niece. But he talked about her all the time...Michelle this, Michelle that."

Then Hemmert wanted to know:

"Did he talk about Michelle coming down here at all, or him going up there?" Skip remembered quickly: "He mentioned that they were gonna go up to his father right before he left work the last time I saw him, and that then they would be staying at Michelle's, is all he said."

Now Hemmert dove right into the core of Charlie's deep desires:

"What other kind of things did he talk about, regarding Michelle?"

"He did mention a boyfriend and how she didn't have much luck with men. He said she was a good-looking woman. She didn't have much luck with men. Something about this latest boyfriend didn't have a car, rode a bicycle, and several other things. And for Charlie to say he doesn't like somebody was more than he usually said, because he was the epitome of that old cliché, 'If you don't have anything good to say, then don't say anything.' So usually you knew when Charlie didn't like something, because he didn't talk about it. But he mentioned this boyfriend and how he didn't think much of him."

Then Hemmert asked another question and received an odd answer: "Did anyone refer to Charlie as anything other than Charlie?" Skip Taylor replied: "His real name is Carl. E. Brandt. And Teri once told me that that sorta morphed from Carl E. to Charlie. And that's just Charlie; he just shrugged it off and accepted Charlie as his name. It was more of a nickname. But a lot of people didn't know Carl was his real name. A lot of people at work didn't know that was his real name."

And then Skip mentioned something curious about Charlie's relationship with Teri that others would allude to again and again. Hemmert had simply asked him, "They were very close then, huh?"

The friend answered, "Yeah, when they were separated Charlie was always talking about her. I'll give you an example. The last time we went to dinner, we drove my 930 Porsche up. We were playing ping-pong and he said he had never been in a Porsche, so I said, 'Let's go for a ride!' So I took him out some of the back roads, got the speeds up pretty good, going around corners, and he was having a really good time. And three or four times he said, 'I wish Teri was here to enjoy this with me.' So that's the kinda, you know, when he wasn't with her he was wishing he was with her. And I noticed if we went out on the boat and she didn't go, she would come up a lot. Most of the time we went out on his boat and it was the four of us. And like uh, right after the first hurricane. One of the other guys, Larry McLane, was leaving, he had a party at his house and Charlie showed up by himself and everyone was like, 'Oh, where's Teri?' Well she was kind of down-in-the-dumps because they had planned a trip, her sisters were coming into town and the hurricane canceled that. So for Charlie to show up to a party without Teri was kind of odd, but he said she was just down-in-the-dumps and kind of upset that she didn't get to see her sisters. But other than that, usually whenever you saw one you saw the other. When they were separated, even if it was just for a few hours, he'd be wishing she was there."

Skip also mentioned that the couple drank a lot. "They were, I guess, what you would call happy drunks. When Teri got over the line she would get laughing. It wasn't bad to be around them. I'd never known Charlie to get trashed—he'd get inebriated, but not trashed. Teri would get trashed but didn't go over the line because he was watching out for her. They drank wine and beer. I don't know what kind of liquor he drank, if he drank liquor at all. I know they liked their beer, he liked his Budweiser, and she liked to drink wine. Out on the boat it was always beer."

And then, the clincher—the one person who not only referred to Charlie as a "sweetheart of a guy," but was in complete denial about his carnage. "I have total disbelief Charlie was part of this," said Skip. My gut feeling is, knowing Charlie, he came upon the scene and was so grief-stricken and he lost it and went and hung himself. But that's my gut feeling. And I know you guys can't say a whole lot, but from what I hear, and knowing Charlie, I can believe when he came home and found that, and realized he couldn't help her, he went out and did it."

Then Skip, remembering an occasion when Charlie refused to lie at work, capped it all by saying, "It was just the kind of person he was. He was honest to a fault. And we're gonna miss him. There's a big hole in the site out there now. I may just quit. I had a hard time the week after it happened. I told my wife, 'I'm going to take this week off and see how it goes', I may not go back out there. It's affected everyone. Everyone has a lot of respect for Charlie."

Everyone?

Al Palladino did. At the end of his interview with the detective, he stated: "Emotionally, it sickens me to sit here and talk to you, because I know what it's about. But intellectually, if it is what it is, why? I'll go to my death saying, 'Why?' I could sit here and praise this guy for hours!"

Hemmert simply said: "I'm sure you could."

Mother Fatally Shot; Teen-Age Son Held

A suburban Fort Wayne mother of four was shot to death about 9 p.m. Sunday, and her husband was seriously wounded. The couple's 13-year-old son, Carl Eric, is being held by Allen County Police on open charges.

Pronounced dead at the scene was Mrs. Ilse L. Brandt, 6208 Stony Brook Drive. She was found by County Police in the bathtub of the home, nude.

The boy is a 9th grade student at Jefferson Junior High School. Police refused to name the youth pending further investigation. The boy has not been charged.

In serious condition today was the father, Herbert, age unknown, reportedly shot three times. It was reported that the father had a collapsed lung and wounds near the heart, left arm, and left side.

Other members of the family include Angela, 15; Jessica, 3, and Melanie, 2.

At a morning press conference, Sheriff Robert Bender said, "We were called to the residence of Mr. and Mrs. Herbert E. Brandt, 6208 Stony Brook Drive, about 9 p.m. and found a woman in a bathtub who had been shot and was apparently dead. We found her husband in a locked bedroom, he had also been shot."

The father was taken to Parkview Memorial Hospital in critical condition and underwent sur-

Related picture on Page 15A

gery about midnight. The sheriff declined to say how many times the father had been shot.

Sheriff Bender said they had talked briefly with the father and would not release the name of the boy. It was found later that the mother was pregnant, Sheriff Bender said.

Public Defender Barrie Tremper was named to represent the boy. Tremper said he had advised the boy of his rights and was being careful to make sure the youth understood.

He said the boy had not been questioned about the incident by County Police and the case will be taken before a juvenile court judge who will determine how to handle the case. Tremper said that this represents a problem since we have no juvenile court judges at present, however it is believed that one will be sworn in by Thursday.

No charges have been filed against the boy. Tremper said he will ask that a mental examination be given the youth before he appears in court.

Sheriff Bender said the youth was the only boy in a family of four children and the remaining

(Turn to Page 1A, Column 6)

Charlie at age 13, the year he killed his pregnant mother. (Courtesy of Tom Pellegrene, Ft. Wayne Journal Gazette)

WHERE SHOOTINGS TOOK PLACE — The Herbert Brandt home, 6208 Stony Brook Drive, was the scene of a double shooting and a death about 9 p.m. Sunday as the Brandt's 13-year-old son allegedly shot his mother to death and seriously wounded his father.

Brandt house in 1973, where the murder took place.

(Courtesy of Tom Pellegrene, Ft. Wayne Journal Gazette)

Newspaper article detailing the murder of then 13 year-old Charlie's pregnant mother. (Courtesy of Tom Pellegrene, Ft. Wayne Journal Gazette)

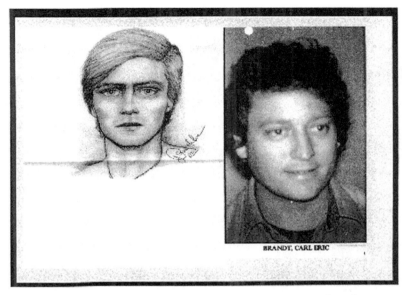

Composite sketch by police artist from eyewitness testimony, describing a man running away from the site of Sherry Perisho's homicide. (Courtesy of Special Agent Leslie D'Ambrosia)

Charlie's class photo at Sea Breeze High School, taken two years after he murdered his mother. (Courtesy of Jim Graves)

Jim Graves class photo at Sea Breeze High School, where he befriended Charlie. (Courtesy of Jim Graves)

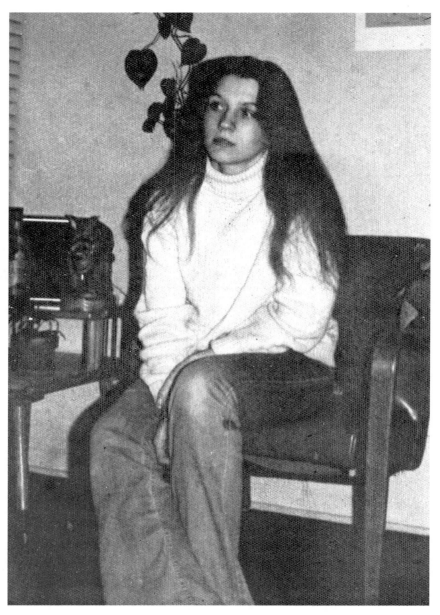

Angela Brandt, Charlie's sister and Jim's ex-wife (Courtesy of Jim Graves)

Angela Brandt with her mother-in-law, Jim's mother Mrs. Graves, Òwho allowed Charlie to stay at her house. (Courtesy of Jim Graves)

Jim and Angie's wedding with Charlie as Best Man. (Courtesy of Jim Graves)

Charlie and Teri Helfrich toasting their new marriage. (Courtesy of Nancy Carney)

First kiss after the wedding. (Courtesy of Nancy Carney)

Charlie and his Best Man Jim after the wedding. (Courtesy of Nancy Carney)

Toasting the newlyweds. L-R: Teri, Charlie, Nancy Carney, Jim. (Courtesy of Nancy Carney)

Teri holding a bouquet after her wedding to Charlie. (Courtesy of Nancy Carney)

Teri and Charlie during a relaxing moment. (Courtesy of Nancy Carney)

A view of Andros Island, where Charlie operated the drug interdiction radar. (Courtesy of Donald Withers)

Charlie in Andros, proud of a fresh big catch.
(Courtesy of Donald Withers)

Sunglow Pier, where Charlie often went fishing. (Courtesy of Donald Withers)

Charlie, Teri, and Nancy in the Keys. (Courtesy of Nancy Carney)

Charlie feeding a deer on his property at Big Pine Key. (Courtesy of Nancy Carney)

A young Sherry Perisho, who lived in her dinghy under the Big Pine Key Bridge. (Courtesy of Marilyn Angel)

Sherry wading in the canal adjacent to the Big Pine Key Bridge. (Courtesy of Special Agent Leslie D'Ambrosia)

Sherry's boat floating upside down under the Big Pine Key Bridge. Charlie had used the boat's bottom as a cutting board to eviscerate her. (Courtesy of Special Agent Leslie D'Ambrosia)

Memorial for Sherry and the other victims by the Monroe County Sheriff's Department. (Courtesy of Marilyn Angel)

Charlie (with back to camera), Teri, and friend's children at the "Swimming Hole" in Big Pine Key, where Sherry often moored her boat. (Courtesy of Special Agent Leslie D'Ambrosia)

Charlie and Teri at a picnic spot at the "Swimming Hole." (Courtesy of Mary Lou Jones)

The Jones Family Christmas during happier times. L-R: Sean, Michelle, Mary Lou, and Bill Jones. (Courtesy of Mary Lou Jones)

Michelle and Teri in Key West. (Courtesy of Mary Lou Jones)

Michelle Jones (center) with her best friends Lisa Emmons (left) and Debbie Wheeler Knight (right) at the Ocean Deck. (Courtesy of Mary Lou Jones)

Charlie (in back), Michelle, Teri, and a group of friends in Key West.
(Courtesy of Suzy Hamilton)

Michelle Jones' house.

Carol Lynn Sullivan, 13, vanished from her school bus stop in Osteen, FL.; Her head was later found inside a paint can. She may have been Brandt's first victim. (From poster for Missing and Exploited Children)

Replica anatomy chart from behind Charlie and Teri's bedroom door. (Courtesy of Special Agent Leslie D'Ambrosia)

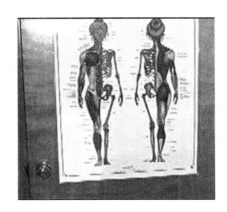

The investigators. L-R: Det. Bob Jaynes, Supervisory Agent John Vecchio, Special Agent and Profiler Leslie D'Ambrosia, Det. Sgt. Dennis Haley, and Det. Rob Hemmert.

IF...

This story is plagued with "ifs:" conjectures, opportunities, and telltale signs missed; avoidable or unavoidable coincidences; and seemingly inevitable unhappy endings, almost like a Greek tragedy. And like a Greek character, be it hero or villain, Charlie Brandt turned out to be larger than life, and wore a mask: a mask of normalcy.

When he had first began to manufacture that mask, it is difficult to say; but what is likely is that he perfected it as he grew up, as he fooled a lot of people—psychiatrists, his own parents, his friends, and ultimately, his wife, her niece, and their friends.

The first "if" occurred on the night of that snowstorm in Fort Wayne, Indiana, when Charlie went upstairs and shot his parents. How did he get access to his father Herbert's Luger, and what would have happened if he had not?

Special Agent Leslie D'Ambrosia has a ready answer, informed by logic: Charlie would have carried out the crimes anyway.

"Yes, I do think he would have sought some other means to accomplish his goal," D'Ambrosia says without hesitation. "His actions were so calculated: to go upstairs, acquire the gun from his father's nightstand in their bedroom, go back downstairs and sit down at the kitchen table and wait—while finishing his homework—and then return to the second floor and shoot his parents. It was so predatory in nature that I think it supports the theory that he had a mission he intended to accomplish. He would have found a way, whether by knife or blunt-force trauma."

As to why Charlie then went after his older sister Angie, tried to shoot her, and when the gun jammed, tried to strangle her and finally pleaded with her not to leave him as they each ran to neighbors' apartments, the profiler attributes it to his being thirteen years old at the time.

"Now, I would surmise that it wasn't a completely sound plan, because he didn't anticipate what to do after that. I attribute that to his age and lack of maturity and criminal sophistication."

When, after his arrest, a police officer asked him: "If your sister would have gotten in your way that night, you think that you would have killed her?" Charlie answered: "It's hard to say. Probably anybody."

It is not certain to anybody whether young Charlie, at that point, was "manipulating the system," as Charles Manson did after he went in and out of reform schools. He might have tried to appear more innocent than he was to the cops, and a "model patient" to the psychiatrists, as Edmund Kemper had. It is hard to say.

What is known is that he did not cry after his father shot his companion dog; that he did not cry at his mother's funeral, which he attended in shackles; and that he did tell his sister Angie that he realized when the mental staff at the hospital expected him to cry.

There is another case besides Edmund Kemper's, in which a killer was released back into society, both by the courts and by accredited medical professionals.

Young Penny Chang's parents emigrated from China to Pittsburgh, Pennsylvania, where Penny was born. They called her Penny because they loved their adopted city and state, but then they relocated to the affluent Shaker Heights section of Ohio, since her father was offered a post as a math professor at Cleveland State University.

Penny and her older brother Sean had friends in common, like twenty-one-year-old Scott Strothers.

Strothers liked Penny. He tried to date her, then pursued her, stalked her, harassed the family mercilessly, and finally, on the morning of March 16, 1999, shot Penny to death, four times in the back, as she walked to school. Strother checked himself into the Cleveland Clinic voluntarily, probably in an effort to avoid a court sentence or parole violation. Later, he wrote that he had checked himself in "because it would look good in court."

The Cleveland Clinic acknowledges that Scott Strothers's date of admission into the emergency room was on October 22, 1998.

According to court documents, his initial diagnosis was listed as "Delusional Disorder vs. Impulse Control Disorder" as well as "Personality Disorder, Not Otherwise Specified."

"Impulse Control Disorder" was the diagnosis, more or less, of Charlie Brandt.

The Cleveland Clinic has since refused to discuss which treatment Strothers received. However, on November 26, 1998, Scott Strothers went home to his family for Thanksgiving.

It is apparent that psychiatrists at the Cleveland Clinic realized that Strothers had homicidal tendencies, and that they were evidently, from the diaries he kept about Penny Chang, directed at one specific young girl.

Strothers, however, from the accounts of all the mental health professionals who gave him the green light to go out into the community and cold-bloodedly murder Penny Chang, was, as so many psychopaths and sociopaths are referred to, "a master manipulator."

Both Scott Strothers and Charlie Brandt had been diagnosed, even if Strothers was much older, as having "an impulse control disorder." Charlie's was termed in a different way, doctors stating that he suffered from "an uncontrollable impulse." What is the difference?

There is no point in casting aspersions on the mental health professionals who felt their patients were no longer a danger to themselves or to others. It is possible that these evil impulses, to call them evil and not "uncontrollable impulses," reach far beyond that. Or that, as Dr. Michael Brannon states, they are undiagnosable because they are "personality disorders."

No one still quite knows the truth about Charlie's parents. It is possible that, without being abusive, they behaved in non-healthy ways towards their children, or at least towards Charlie. Nobody ever knows what happens behind closed doors. And Charlie told psychiatrists and investigators he "loved" his parents.

In his informed investigation of human evil, "*People of the Lie*," M. Scott Peck posits, "When a child is grossly confronted by significant evil in its parents, it will most likely misinterpret the situation and believe that the evil resides in itself."

But then Peck qualifies this carefully:

"Does evil run in families because it is genetic and inherited? Or because it is learned by the child in imitation of its parents? Or even as a defense against its parents? And how are we to explain the fact that the children of evil parents, although usually scarred, are not evil? We do not know, and we will not know until an enormous amount of painstaking scientific work has been accomplished."

There is also no point in wondering what would have happened if Jim had told Teri about Charlie's past. "I don't blame myself for that one," he said. "What I blame myself for is that time when I was playing a gig at Hammerhead's and Teri came to me with the story about Charlie covered in blood in the fish-cleaning room."

That had been, of course, right after the murder and evisceration of Sherry Perisho under the Big Pine Key Bridge, a few blocks from Charlie and Teri's house. Jim does not blame himself for not fessing up about Charlie's past, because he made Charlie swear he would tell Teri, and also because of what Angela had said to Teri: "You know everything about him and you love him anyway?" And there was another time he'd asked Teri, "When are you going to have kids?" and she answered, "We're not going to have kids, considering." Jim assumed it was considering Charlie's past, which is a sound assumption, although Teri's sister and Michelle's mother, Mary Lou Jones, disagrees. "It might have been because Teri was there for the birth of all of her nephews and nieces." But that doesn't jell with Teri saying "considering."

Melanie Fecher, Teri's best friend on the Key, also disagrees:

"Both of us had talked about not wanting to have children," Melanie said. "That is probably what she meant."

As to why Jim did not encourage Teri to go to the sheriff, as she'd wanted to do, when she found Charlie covered in blood in the fish-cleaning room, he stated, again, that he did feel most sorry and saddened about that. "It was the first real gig I'd had in awhile, and the music was loud, and there was no time, and we had all been drinking, and it just didn't make any sense." He was, of course, referring to the violent butchering of Sherry Perisho, although Jim did not know it at the time.

But then, the Monroe County Sheriff's Office also fell a few blocks short in seeking out Sherry Perisho's killer. One of the most efficient and persistent police departments in the State of Florida, they canvassed the neighborhood door to door, looking for neighbors who might have been witnesses to the carnage inflicted on the popular, harmless resident who lived in her dinghy.

The canvass stopped when authorities brought in a profiler who narrowed down the suspect as a homeless transient, jobless and having no family. The police brought in every homeless transient and the neighborhood canvassing stopped. What might have happened if they had gone two doors? Would Teri have told them the story about Charlie in the fish-cleaning room covered in blood? Again, nobody will ever know.

There were always signs with Charlie. Several people referred to "the glazed look" that came over his eyes at times. The first was Angela when he tried to strangle her and she was able to dispel his "glazed, maniacal look." When the two siblings then went running to neighbors' homes, knocking frantically on their doors, Angie asking for shelter and Charlie saying he had done "something bad," the neighbor who opened her door to Charlie remembers "he had the blackest eyes I had ever seen."

Bill Jones, Michelle father, referred to that change in Charlie as well. "One time we were having lobsters and he had a glazed look in his eyes. I said, 'Charlie, are you okay?' and he snapped right out of it and said, 'Oh yeah...yeah."

And what about Michelle Jones? What if she had decided to leave her home on that night when she'd said Teri and Charlie were arguing, and "it wasn't very pleasant"? She could have gotten into her car and gone to meet Lisa Emmons, the friend who was late. Of course Michelle, who was so careful of her image and protective of her job, would never have gotten into her car if she'd had even a couple of drinks.

Colleen Maloney met Teri at the University of Southern Mississippi.

Colleen was one of many young enthusiastic students taking in the fresh atmosphere of college life at the University of Southern Mississippi. Here, she thought, was a chance to finally make something out of independence. New friends and new experiences lay waiting to reveal themselves, like unopened Christmas presents. When unwrapped, one proved to be the best gift of all: a true friend.

Teri Helfrich was an outgoing, quick-with-a-comeback, lighthearted student who was enjoyed by almost everyone who met her. A mutual friend of Colleen's roommate led to Colleen and Teri being introduced and becoming best friends; friends who would grow apart geographically, but not personally or, most importantly, at the heart.

"We got to be friends through one of my roommates, and eventually she became my best friend," Colleen said about Teri.

Then a beacon of light known as the Sunshine State called Teri's name, and she decided to embark on her journey to Florida.

The career calling baited Colleen in, and she proceeded to successfully fill a position with a local hotel management company that conveniently owned several properties—most importantly, properties that were in Florida. With a free place to stay, Colleen took every opportunity to travel to Daytona Beach and see Teri; one trip provided the message that would change everything.

Strangely enough, at first it seemed as though there could not be a better piece of personal news. Teri explained how she had met someone who had not only the same interests as her, but also was the most genuine, man she had ever met. Colleen was thrilled for Teri, who seemed to have found the one thing almost everyone yearns for in this life—someone to spend the rest of her life with. If only at the time Teri had realized that the man known by the name Charlie was only disguising the devil inside him, freely passing out the drug known as deception.

"Every chance I got to see Teri, I would," her friend Colleen said. "During one of the trips to Daytona Beach at the time, Teri told me about meeting someone, and it was Charlie. She was on cloud nine. She felt she had finally met someone who had the same interests she did, and he was such a good person." If only Colleen had known.

As time passed, Colleen fell deep into a relationship with a man nick-named "Fish," which would later build into a marriage in January of 1990. It was during this time (corroborated by Teri's daily planner) that both Teri and Charlie had traveled to Jackson, Mississippi, to help their good friends, with whom they had spent many happy occasions, celebrate their upcoming marriage. It was during this time that an incident would occur that only years later in hindsight would prove of any relevance.

The night before Colleen went from being Colleen Maloney to Colleen Maloney Michie, she had thrown her bachelorette party and in an attempt to have a night out of his own, "Fish" Michie decided to take Charlie out to a local bar where he played piano. It was a typical night at the bar. Fish finished playing, and after he'd put away his equipment, the men shared conversations, put back beers, and looked towards both of their prospective futures. A man walked past the crowded space Charlie and Fish were occupying, and while the nudge was minor and uninten-tional, Charlie reacted. "But when Charlie turned around and looked at my husband," Colleen said, "something very strange happened, and my husband never reacts like that!" Charlie turned around and sent a soul-shivering stab down Fish's spine.

Fish remembered that Charlie was kind of loose, since they had both been drinking at Kristo's, the piano bar where Fish played jazz. "But he wasn't a belligerent drunk, he was sort of slow," Colleen's husband recalls.

"I remember it was after my gig, and I was packing up my equip-ment, and Charlie was going to help me, and a guy bumped into him. I saw Charlie turn and look at this guy, and I saw Charlie's eyes and it was chilling! He had shark eyes! The blackest eyes, without expression. I said, 'It's okay, it's okay.' He didn't acknowledge me. When he turned around and looked at that guy, my blood ran cold."

The blackness was indeed like looking into the eyes of a great white shark that understood the emotional repercussions of its hunting—what every bite, every tear of flesh, every drop of blood meant as a whole and how that pain and destruction could bring the greatest pleasure to the hunter.

Years later, when the *48 Hours* program was aired, briefly summarizing Charlie Brandt's life, the producers interviewed the neighbor who had opened the door to the haunted thirteen-year-old after he had "done something bad." She described this little kid by saying, "He had the blackest eyes I had ever seen!"

Charlie's eyes were blue.

The musician married to one of Teri's best friends noticed something else about Charlie's eyes. It was the "glazed look" several people have noticed, but Fish Michie sensed something more. "I thought he was into drugs because he would get a glazed look in his eyes sometimes. Even after a couple of drinks, I felt he got immersed in something. I can't put my finger on it." Obviously Fish, with more instinct than most, perceived something sinister, an inner world of perverse imaginings. There can be no doubt that is where Charlie was going, when he turned his gaze inwards.

Fish remembered another instance that coincided with other stories told by others.

"We live in Marigold, Mississippi. The weekend I asked Colleen to marry me, Teri and Colleen went shopping at Greenville, which is about thirty miles away. They said they'd be back in an hour. An hour went by and Charlie got nasty, and started pacing around and cursing. Then another hour went by, and he became like a child, whining, 'Where is Teri? What did Colleen do with Teri?'"

If Teri was another part of his mask of normalcy, Charlie must have felt exposed, almost naked, like a babe in the woods, when she was not by his side.

Fish remembered another incident when Charlie became childlike.

"One time, in the Keys, we grabbed a little fourteen-foot boat to go across to a restaurant. On the way back across, everyone had been drinking and Charlie kept saying, like a kid, 'We're not going home, we're floating out to the Gulf! Where do we live, Teri, where do we live?' It was entirely too creepy. And now I think, he could have killed me and Colleen that night!" And maybe sometimes Charlie simply regressed and returned back to the night of January 3, 1971.

Fish remembered how it all was at first, when he began dating Colleen and he met Teri. "Everyone kept saying, 'You have to meet Charlie, he's the greatest guy!' And I thought that for a long time, until that night at Kristo's when I saw his eyes. Nobody had a clue!"

Apparently, Fish had more of a clue than anyone else.

Lisa Emmons, an outspoken, articulate, and attractive blonde and one of Michelle's best friends, remembers, and she calls it that, "the glazed look." "I thought it was because he smoked a lot of pot," Lisa said. It was corroborated that Charlie did smoke marijuana, and also took LSD and other psychedelic drugs. But Lisa had one experience with Charlie she has not forgotten.

She recalled a club she and Michelle and Charlie and Teri, when they were in town, used to frequent in Central Florida, near Altamonte Springs.

"There used to be a club at Lake Fairview," she began. "We were twenty-three years old." Lisa continued in vivid detail.

A full moon illuminated the volleyball tournament that had been carrying on from earlier in the afternoon. The shores of Lake Fairview, in Altamonte Springs just outside the heart of Central Florida, were filled with partiers flowing in and out of the doors of "Shooters." There was seafood, outside decks, live music, and plenty of alcohol to lubricate the awkwardness of sober social interaction.

In the midst of this whirlwind of activity was a party of four: Michelle Jones, her friend Lisa Emmons, Teri, and Charlie. Anytime Charlie and Teri had made their way into town from their home down in the Keys, the group would get together at the lake for drinks and for the girls to play catch-up in the conversation department. Charlie never said much.

"Down the road I saw odd things," Teri's college roommate and friend, Colleen Maloney Michie had said. "Charlie wanted to be around Teri so much; he seemed too needy. I don't know if that's because she was with me, or an insecurity type of thing."

The incident brings back the time when thirteen-year-old Charlie pleaded with his sister, Angela, right after he shot his mother to death and critically wounded his father, "Promise me you won't leave me!"

Colleen recalled a particular time.

"My husband and I were just dating at the time. We would travel with Teri and Charlie to the Keys and they came to Mississippi for our wedding. This time we all traveled to Mexico, to Cozumel. We were at a bar, and Teri went to the restroom. Charlie looked at us and said, very meekly and sadly, 'I miss Teri.' I said, 'Charlie, she's in the bathroom, get over it!' I just took that as, he's different."

This is reminiscent of the time when Charlie, age thirteen, asked his older sister Angela, after shooting their mother to death, "Promise me you won't leave me?" Did Charlie have a fear of abandonment? Did he see

Teri more like a sister than a wife? At one point, during that awful night of January 3, 1971, Charlie had tried to kill his sister.

It is known he was left alone by his father when Herbert remarried and left him in the care of his grandparents, but what happened when he was thirteen and he shot his mother? Was it on account of her pregnancy?

Charlie would follow several people throughout his life. Why he followed Lisa Emmons, Michelle's friend, as she was swimming, nobody will know, but his intentions were certainly not good.

It was around 11 o' clock, and Lisa Emmons had decided to sneak away for a swim in the lake. She was knowledgeable of the water and knew that alligators were always awaiting a new feast, so she cut her way through the lily pads and walked through the muddy banks. Two eyes followed.

The water rippled with every move Lisa made, her body a point sending energy in all directions. It was a peaceful scenario for her—a few moments alone from the noise of the crowd and a refreshing way to clear her head. Two eyes watched. Thoughts of water moccasins began to creep into Lisa's head not too far along into the swim. The Florida snakes could shoot venom up the arteries with one deathblow. These reptilian visions sent Lisa into a quick rush back up the bank.

She struggled to get to her feet along the marsh but as she regained her footing and hoisted herself up, she was met by the face of a predator far more lethal than any snake. His eyes glazed over, absent of anything outside of obsession, and peered into Lisa's, as if holding some dark mystery. Her heart began to race and cold bumps raised up on her skin. All this time she thought she had been alone. She finally began to speak and asked the only thing she could manage to verbalize.

"Charlie, what are you doing here?" He did not say a word.

Two eyes stared, leaving an imprint on the young woman's mind that she would never be able to erase.

"Sometimes he was really odd," Lisa said as an afterthought. "But that was the creepiest time ever. He never even offered to help. I have no idea how he got there, but he snapped away from everyone else, in the dark of night."

Nancy Carney, Teri's former roommate and good friend, remembered another instance where a woman was accosted more directly by Charlie.

Teri and Charlie were inseparable. That is the warm exterior that they presented. Whether it was traveling together, having dinner with friends, or out for a drink, they would always be seen right next to one another, in some photos arm in arm, hand in hand. But below the surface of this façade were the icy and erratic undercurrents coldly calculated like some matrix destined to be only fully understood by its creator, a creator of lies and a destroyer of lives. The creator was Charlie Brandt. Did he want Teri, gullible Teri, as his partner in apparent perfection?

Maybe he did not even love her after they were married.

Nancy, the woman who was responsible for the initial introduction of Charlie and Teri, had finished packing her things and picked up her friend Lesa Cravey. It was a trip they had planned, and like so many other times, the trip would entail partying in the Keys with the Brandts. It was a fairly straight shot of a drive, and with the windows down, the sun blared down on the two young women as they pummeled the I-95 South pavement all the way to the South Florida Turnpike, over the famous 7-Mile Bridge and into Key West. They also were unknowingly already playing into the puzzle in Charlie's mind.

One evening, the foursome, Charlie and Teri and Nancy and Lesa, headed out to the Tiki Lounge nearby. Nancy found herself enjoying the conversation of a man she had met earlier in the night. The group spent the first few hours downing tequila shots with beer chasers, and Teri at this point had pushed herself to the point of inebriation, Charlie had explained to both Nancy and Lesa that he was going to take Teri back to the house, and that they should feel free to join them. Nancy decided to stick around for a few more hours. She wasn't drunk, after all. Lesa had decided to call it an evening. The next day the two friends departed the Brandt house on their way back to Daytona Beach, both carrying a smile—and one of them carrying a secret.

Time and time again Nancy would make the same routine trip, every time inviting Lesa to join her; yet for some odd reason, Lesa would decline. Nancy wondered what was wrong with her longtime traveling companion, but never could seem to get an answer. Lesa spoke up after the crimes.

"Nancy and I went there; they were friends of Nancy's whom I never met," said Nancy's friend. "It was Memorial Day weekend. It was the end of May 1990. We went there on a Friday night, got there kind of late. Next morning we had breakfast, went out on the boat, and they were a nice couple, as sweet as they could be!" Then Lesa Cravey said something others had said as well: "We spent the weekend, and Charlie was the designated driver."

She went on: "We went to a place close to home, stopped at a tiki bar, stayed there for a while, and Nancy was not coming home with us. Teri went into the bedroom. Charlie and I were in the living room, and he asked me if he could kiss me. I said, 'Charlie what are you talking about, Teri is Nancy's friend! And she is sleeping in the other room!' Again he asked if he could kiss me, and I talked my way out of it. It freaked me out at the time, because Nancy had told me about this couple that adored each other. I didn't tell Nancy for a long time because Teri was her best friend, and she had this idea. I told him, 'No, this would ruin my friendship with Nancy.'"

As Nancy said, Lesa never went back to Big Pine Key to Teri and Charlie's house with her again. "Every time she went back I always had an excuse not to go. She finally cornered me and asked me, 'Why won't you go back?' And I told her very briefly that he had made a pass at me. Nancy was very upset."

Lesa said that it didn't bother her so much at the time, since married men had done that before and she'd rebuked them successfully. "But after the murders happened, I thought, What if? Why me? What did I do?" She did not know Charlie had come onto other women.

"When Nancy did tell me about what happened, I couldn't believe it!" Lesa offered. "They seemed a perfectly happy couple until he made a pass at me. It freaks me out when I heard about the woman he'd killed right before we went down there." Lesa was referring to Sherry Perisho, whom Charlie murdered in 1989.

It was through these words that Nancy got to take a look into a matrix so carefully constructed by Charlie; and through Brandt's own actions that Lesa got to have a brief glimpse at the monster behind the mask

Some people believed Charlie was very lovey-dovey with Teri, waiting on her hand-and-foot at parties. Lisa Emmons, thought it was because he never wanted to participate.

Melanie Fecher, Teri's best friend on Big Pine Key, remembered pretty much the same thing.

"No matter where we went, the women would sit together, and Teri would sit by Charlie. He was always asking, 'Where is Teri? Where is Teri?' We would say, 'Charlie, she just went to the bathroom!'

Charlie first expressed this fear of abandonment to his older sister, Angela, after he had shot their mother and wounded their father. He said to her at the time, "Promise me you won't leave me!" What did this mean? Again, probably, we will never know. It was this fear of abandonment that had been the trigger for Jeffrey Dahmer to keep the body parts of his male lovers.

Lisa Emmons, Michelle Jones's friend, also thought Teri harbored thoughts of divorcing Charlie.

"When they came up here for Hurricane Ivan, I had talked to Teri, because my divorce started August 27, 2004, and they came in September. Michelle had told Teri I had just filed for divorce. I talked to Teri on the phone much earlier, late afternoon I would say. Charlie was grilling fish. I believe they were making margaritas. They were not getting along at that time.

"Teri knew I had just started the divorce process. I can remember Teri saying, 'I'm considering divorce, too, Lisa. I want to move away from the Keys, I'm just tired of this laid-back lifestyle; I want something more to my life.' Lisa had asked Teri why she could not just move to the mainland. She could hear Charlie talking to Michelle in the background, about the fish. "Well, Charlie is just adamant about not leaving the Keys," Teri had said with despair in her voice. "He just wants to stay there and stagnate. We're just growing apart, that's all."

Lisa remembered, "Teri really wanted to talk to me about what it was like, the divorce process. She said it wasn't definite, but that she was thinking about it. She said Charlie was becoming unmotivated, and he wasn't growing with her."

Was that how the argument escalated? Lisa did not hear anymore, until the time she was in her car going over to Michelle's for dinner and she was running late. And Michelle told her not to bother, that Teri and Charlie were drinking and arguing.

And some time after that, it happened.

Melanie Fecher, Teri's best friend on Big Pine Key, also remembered:

"A couple of months before the murders, Teri was very depressed because she didn't have a job, and Charlie said, "If she doesn't straighten out, I'm going to get a divorce."

Mary Lou, Teri's sister and Michelle's mother, said Teri had expressed her dissatisfaction on more than one occasion a few months before the murders.

Charlie had told Mary Lou, and several other people, that his mother had died in a car accident. "When someone says that, you don't pry," said Mary Lou, who is very polite and respectful of others' privacy. "But in the spring of 2004, Teri was very despondent and wanted to move to the mainland. That was whenever she and I talked, several months prior to September 4. She not only said she wanted to relocate to the mainland, but also pointed out that Charlie's work opportunities were limited because of the type of work he did. I remember that, on a number of occasions, when we would say good-bye at the end of the conversation, she had a catch in her voice, like she was going to cry. I did ask her about that, but she denied being upset. After her death, this is one of the areas I continued to reflect on. Perhaps he wanted to keep Teri isolated. And after the murders we did learn that one of his co-workers had been terminated from the company after he had been discovered to be involved with drugs."

What would have happened if Teri had moved out? By her sister's account, she seemed so depressed as to be almost resigned and immobilized.

M. Scott Peck seems to corroborate this in *"People of the Lie"* by explaining the relationship between an evil person and a healthy one:

"The feeling that a healthy person often experiences in a relationship with an evil one is revulsion. The feeling of revulsion may be almost instant if the evil encountered is blatant. If the evil is more subtle, the revulsion may develop only gradually as the relationship with the evil one slowly deepens."

According to investigators, when Charlie and Teri evacuated their large house in Big Pine Key because of Hurricane Ivan, everything was boarded to perfection, to specification—even the wood around the door handles was cut in perfect circles. The home was also spotless and orderly. And Charlie did seem like a model husband. But here's the rub, according to Peck:

"There is another reaction that the evil frequently engender in us:

confusion. Describing her encounter with an evil person, one woman wrote, it was 'as if I'd suddenly lost the ability to think.' Once again, the reaction is quite appropriate. Lies confuse. The evil are 'the people of the lie', deceiving others as they also build layer upon layer of self-deception."

If Teri was confused and despondent, perhaps the urgency of surviving the hurricane and going to visit her beloved niece provided a little spark, a bit of hope. Also, she was looking forward to her upcoming chat with Lisa Emmons about Lisa's divorce.

And if one considers Teri's entries in her daily planner, it is evident that it is filled with despondency and fear.

And what if Lisa Emmons had gone on to Michelle's house, as she'd briefly considered? Would she have been able to divert the massacre? It is doubtful, since a violent argument was already in progress.

"As I look back on how weird Charlie was that night," Lisa recalled the evening she went swimming in the dark when the girls were twenty-three, "if I didn't have my wits about me, judging from the look on his face, I could be dead."

Lisa had been right on the corner, close to Michelle's house during the murders. She had keys to the house. She said the music inside was blaring really loudly, and they would not have heard anybody knocking. Lisa thought of letting herself in, but she did not.

"Michelle was the most awesome person ever. My life is not complete since she's not here," her friend reminisced. That night, she added, "my keys got the cops inside the house, but they would not let anyone else in. There were helicopters flying overhead, and Debbie was already there before me, and she knew everything. She knew Charlie was dead."

And what about Debbie Knight? What if she hadn't left early Sunday morning and stayed for the entire weekend like the two friends had planned? Debbie was not unlike Michelle. She had the same body type and was also an attractive young woman. Surely he would have taken her with him, and it is probably what he had planned.

Lisa remembered she was standing outside Michelle's house for hours, along with Debbie. "When they put spotlights on in Michelle's garage, from where I was sitting I could see the silhouette of Charlie's body swinging. Then it hit me like a ton of bricks. Realizing he was evil and that night he followed me to the lake he was up to no good."

Jim Graves admitted that, if he could go back and do everything over, "I would make sure Teri knew about Charlie's mother. After seeing the gunshots wounds on his father Herbert's back when I visited with Angie that time, I went to my mom and dad and I said, 'I don't know what to do here.' They said, 'If you like him, and he's a good friend, then leave it as a youngster who made a bad decision, and leave it be.' If I could take anything back it would be telling Teri not to call the cops after the girl was murdered in Big Pine Key. I wondered for a long time if that was the right thing to do. I am also convinced in my heart that he killed that girl in Astor. He would have been living at my mom's house at the time, but her house was right down Highway 40; it's not too much of a stretch to Astor."

As to what would have been the outcome had Charlie not killed himself, that does seem like the only inevitable conclusion.

Both employers and authorities would have known about his not only botching the drug interdiction operation, but turning it into a drug-dealing business, and taking the drugs himself. Who knows if they might have found out about Andros Island?

It is altogether possible that before his final exit he'd planned on enjoying himself. He wanted Michelle; that is a known fact. The fight with his wife Teri was yet another precipitator.

And his suicide pointed to his knowledge. As Detective Diaz stated simply, "He knew that the jig was up."

As to the question of whether Charlie was born evil, Diaz is unequivocal.

"Evil? Absolutely. He never got rehabilitation. That anger stayed with him as part of his life. Once a killer, always a killer. He had deep, dark secrets."

Lisa Emmons, Michelle's friend who encountered Charlie at the lake all those years ago, concurs. "Afterwards I realized he was purely evil, and he meant me harm that night," she said.

Debbie Knight, from the psychic Rosemary Altea's account and from her own writings, agrees. "I encountered pure evil," Debbie says, remembering the violent brush with his spirit.

One might think Special Agent, Leslie D'Ambrosia, with all of her years in law enforcement and looking into the hearts of serial killers, would have another explanation.

D'Ambrosia did hesitate before drawing a conclusion, but then stated, "Evil? I cannot answer with any support. I have an opinion and I think he was devoid of feeling anything real for others. This was exhibited from an early age. Is that something he was born with? That is a topic argued by academicians and psychiatrists, et cetera, for a long time. It can be a combination of genetics and environment, but we don't know. 'Evil' is a descriptive word not based in genetics or science, so saying he was 'born evil' is an opinion—one I'm sure many have for Charlie.

"I found no information to indicate he suffered any abuse or trauma in his life. So his environment was good. The worst thing I heard he had experienced was that he wasn't too happy about moving to Indiana. So do I personally think he was evil? For the record, yes. How could I not?"

The biggest "if," is still, of course, the murder and evisceration of Sherry Perisho under the Big Pine Key Bridge in 1989.

It was only after the murders of Teri Helfrich Brandt and Michelle Jones, and Charlie's suicide, that Sergeant Dennis Haley and Special Agent Leslie D'Ambrosia went back to review the case of Sherry Perisho.

What follows is the official police report:

On October 5, 2004, Special Agent Edward Royal and Special Agent Leslie D'Ambrosia met with Special Agent Dennis Haley, FDLE Key West Office, and members of the Monroe County Sheriff's Office Homicide Unit in Marathon, Florida. A briefing was provided by Det. Sgt. Patricia Dally and Detective James Norman, concerning the unsolved homicide of Sherry

Irene Perisho that had occurred in 1989.

The purpose of the meeting was to gather information for an assessment of the linkage of the Perisho homicide to a double murder/suicide that had occurred in Seminole County, Florida, in September 2004.

It was reported that Carl Eric Brandt and his wife Teri Brandt had traveled to Maitland, Florida, from the Florida Keys in September 2004, to escape Hurricane Ivan, projected to strike the state.

The Brandts evacuated to the residence of Teri Brandt's niece, Michelle Lynn Jones, on September 15, 2004. The bodies of all three were discovered on Monday, September 20, 2004, when the Brandts did not return to work in the Florida Keys.

Teri Brandt was discovered deceased on the sofa with a stab wound to the chest area.

Michelle Jones was discovered deceased in her bed. She had been decapitated and her head was placed beside her torso on the bed. She was eviscerated; some internal organs had been removed and placed inside a wastebasket nearby. Her heart had been removed. Her breasts had been cut off and were placed nearby. Her leg also had been disarticulated. There was underwear belonging to Jones in the bedroom, which had been cut on one side. Carl "Charlie" Brandt was found in the garage hanging by a bedsheet, deceased as a result of suicide.

The Monroe County Sheriff's Office requested a comparison of the Perisho homicide to the Brandt/Jones homicides. The Brandts had resided on Big Pine Key in the Florida Keys since 1986.

In 1989, Sherry Perisho's body was discovered in the water on Big Pine Key. She had been eviscerated and her heart had been removed. Her head had been severed to the spinal column. She was discovered floating in the water near the Big Pine Channel Bridge. Her boat was overturned and was nearby. It was reported that the victim was discovered at approximately 10:15 p.m. by a person fishing in the area. It was determined that she had only been in the water for a short period of time.

Perisho was a homeless resident who lived in a dinghy-type boat along *the Big Pine Channel on the south side of the Big Pine Channel Bridge. The Brandts resided in a residential neighborhood on Big Pine Key located on the north side of the Big Pine Channel Bridge a very short distance from the crime scene.*

FLORIDA DEPARTMENT OF LAW ENFORCEMENT
INVESTIGATIVE REPORT
Case Number: MI-73-1157 Serial #:1
Author: D'Ambrosia, Leslie
Office: Miami
Activity Start Date: 10/05/2004 Activity End Date: 10/05/2004
Approved By: Browdy, Shirley B.
Description: Meeting with Monroe County SO re: Perisho homicide

On this same date, the above mentioned individuals responded to the Brandt residence on Big Pine Key.

A viewing of the interior and exterior of the Brandt residence was conducted. An on-site viewing of the former Perisho crime scene was also conducted.

Det. Sgt. Dally advised that the Monroe County Sheriff's Office had collected several items from the Brandt residence and had turned the items over to the Seminole County Sheriff's Office.

Among some of the items were diaries or agenda books of Teri Brandt, Carl Brandt's computer, and miscellaneous photographs and papers. An anatomical chart had previously been discovered on the backside of the master bedroom door. The chart depicted the muscular and skeletal systems of a female.

SA D'Ambrosia maintained contact with Special Agent Tom Davis of the Melbourne, Florida FDLE Office regarding this case. SA Davis was previously contacted by the Seminole County Sheriff's Office regarding this investigation.

Det. Sgt. Dally requested a crime scene assessment/linkage comparing the Seminole County crime to the Perisho homicide.

On Wednesday, October 6, 2004 Special Agents Leslie D'Ambrosia and Edward Royal met with Monroe County Sheriff's Office (MCSO) Sergeant James Norman in an effort to determine the location, where a Polaroid photograph was taken of what appears to be Sherry Perisho. That photograph was located in the MCSO case file and it shows a female sitting on a concrete wall along the edge of a canal, which looks very similar to the canal on which Teri and Charles Brandt resided in Big Pine Key, Florida.

The photograph had to have been taken before July 19, 1989, which was the date that Perisho's body was found along the edge of the channel, less than a quarter of a mile from the Brandt residence.

Sergeant Norman escorted SA D'Ambrosia and SA Royal to various waterways along the southern tip of Big Pine Key, including the "Brandts'" canal. The entire area has undergone a great deal of change in the past fifteen years and after visiting several locations, a determination could not be made as to where that photograph was taken.

On October 6, 2004, Special Agent Dennis Haley, SA Edward Royal and SA Leslie D'Ambrosia responded to the Monroe County Sheriff's Office and met with Det. Sgt. Patricia Dally, Det. James Norman, and Det. Trisha Almeda concerning the unsolved homicide of Sherry Irene Perisho.

Det. Trisha Almeda advised that she was responsible for the crime-scene processing on the Perisho case. She allowed the above individuals to view Perisho's boat and made her case reports available for review. It was noted that the boat had scratches on the bottom portion, consistent with the offender cutting the victim on this surface, according to Almeda. Additionally, Det. Almeda advised that she noted in her report that green paint chips were recovered from the neck wound of the victim. This would also be consistent with the victim having been placed on top of the overturned boat when her neck was cut. The bottom of the boat was painted green.

SA Royal noted that an unidentified fingerprint of AFIS quality was recovered from a beer can on the victim's boat. The fingerprint had been discovered by the Broward Sheriff's Office, who performed some of the analysis *of evidence in this case. SA Haley noted the laboratory case numbers for reference to FDLE laboratory analysis. SA Haley advised he would research the results of the FDLE laboratory analysis.*

And what if Charlie had not hung himself from the rafters inside Michelle's garage after the murders? Would either the investigators or the families have gotten the answers as to his motives? The answer to the first "if" is that Charlie's suicide was almost inevitable. As for the answers, it is doubtful as to whether even Charlie knew why he committed all of his crimes.

M. Scott Peck might attribute Charlie's final curtain on his acting to the expenditure of sheer psychic energy and the fear he experienced. "Think of the amount of psychic energy required for the continuing maintenance of the pretense so characteristic of evil! They perhaps direct at least as much energy into their devious rationalizations and destructive compensations as the healthiest do into loving behavior. Why? What possesses them, drives them? Basically, it is fear. They are terrified that the pretense will break down and they will be exposed to the world and to themselves. They are continually frightened that they will come face-to-face with their own evil." Charlie Brandt was finally faced with his own fear.

For her part, Mary Lou Jones, psychiatric nurse, sister, and mother, has her own theory:

"I believe he had a covert evil nature, and I believe he was able to control it and cover it. He was an invisible killer."

WARDING OFF EVIL

Shortly after their daughter's death, Bill and Mary Lou Jones set up the Michelle Lynn Jones Foundation.

"It outlined three initiatives, and they all moved in a positive direction," Mary Lou stated, and then added, "The mission statement is on our website."

The website can be found at http://www.mlj-foundation.org.

And indeed, the website for the Michelle Lynn Jones Foundation lists its history, mission statements, and initiatives as follows:

HISTORY

During the subsequent investigation of Michelle and Teri's gruesome murders, the discovery was made that Carl Brandt had murdered before. He took the life of his mother, attempted to murder his father and then tried to kill his older sister thirty three years earlier in Fort Wayne, Indiana, when he was thirteen years old.

Although he was never convicted of a crime, the Grand Jury conducting the investigation summarized their concerns with a message stating that Carl Brandt should be closely monitored, as they feared he might repeat this crime. Intervention at the time was to place Carl Brandt in a state mental hospital for one year, after holding him in the county jail for four months. In July 1972, Carl Brandt was released from the state mental hospital. Diagnosis: no longer mentally ill.

In 1986, Charlie Brandt married Teri Helfrich in Ormond Beach, Florida. Within the year, they relocated to the Florida Keys where they lived until their deaths. Throughout the discovery of Michelle and Teri's murders those who knew Charlie were shocked and in disbelief—that is, until the secret of Charlie's murder of his mother, and attempted murder of his father and older sister, were made public by his older sister.

Yes, an "invisible criminal" had lived among us for all the years we had known him.

OUR MISSION

The mission of the Michelle Lynn Jones Foundation is to promote personal safety by raising public awareness about invisible criminals in our communities through public education and advocacy and enhanced education for health care professionals and law enforcement, enabling law enforcement to conduct more comprehensive criminal investigations, as needed.

These major initiatives will require time and your support to process and achieve the intended outcomes.

EDUCATION
PROTECTED DATABASE
PUBLIC AWARENESS
FIRST INITIATIVE —Enhanced education of the clinical/scientific community, educators, law enforcement and the judicial system, related to the egregious nature of violent crimes committed by juveniles, such as murder or attempted murder. The focus is on the long-term implications for individuals and families when these crimes are erased. Where do these criminals go? Who do these criminals become? Moreover, the additional effort with this education is to address the effects of keeping these crimes a secret from those who may be adversely affected because of this action.

Mary Lou Jones, who holds a Doctorate degree, explained that these were areas of focus. "Once we conducted our investigation and did a thorough background of what happened, we tried to figure out how that affected our world and what we needed to do about it. We needed to raise awareness that there are people walking around us who have very dark natures; we need to be aware of this and ask questions.

"We want to educate the health care community that there are juvenile criminals who are not rehabilitated, and there need to be mechanisms."

Mary Lou then reached out to Dr. Sally Johnson, a psychiatrist who had been a family practitioner, who taught in the Psychiatry Department at the University of North Carolina.

Mary Lou Jones and Dr. Johnson met in Dr. Johnson's kitchen, since she was already retired and no longer an office. "We spent the whole morning around her kitchen table," Michelle's proactive mother explained. "I told Sally, 'I am asking for any suggestions you have about educating the health care community. We had a person who was a criminal in our midst for eighteen years and we didn't know. And his father knew and his sister knew. I don't believe for a minute that if my sister had known she would have married him.'"

Dr. Johnson thought it was too soon after Teri and Michelle's deaths to formulate any plan, but she did think it would be helpful to hold a panel about juvenile criminals.

"Juvenile criminals are put into juvenile homes," Mary Lou said. "If they are incarcerated, it is until they reach the age of eighteen, and their records are expunged. Dr. Johnson offered to convene a panel of child and juvenile psychologists under the umbrella title, 'Juvenile Offenders Challenges and Dispositions.' That meeting was held in October, 2004, at the American Academy of Psychiatry and the Law in Chicago, Illinois—international meeting, which is known by the acronym, The APPLE Group."

Mary Lou explained: "They clearly presented the challenges of juveniles who commit a crime and are treated and become productive citizens. However, there is a population that is not, that cannot be rehabilitated."

Mary Lou spoke to some people in several states who mentioned assessment tools that are particular indicators for remorse. "What they have discovered is, if the juvenile shows no remorse, he or she has a high likelihood of reoffending."

Mary Lou firmly believes that there are limits to the rehabilitation of some juveniles. The problem is that they might not be retained, either in the jail or mental health system, until they reach the age of adulthood.

"In the adult world, if someone is incarcerated and there are concerns about their behavior, they can retain them beyond their sentence. With the juveniles, they are released and they expunge those records."

As to public records and prior criminal records, Mary Lou believes that before the Internet, Google, Facebook, and MySpace and other social media, the expunging of records might have been a concern, whereas now it might not be such a priority.

"Right now you can find out about an individual, so that area of concern is probably not as important," she said. "The other area is interacting with the law enforcement community, and Sheriff Don Eslinger and Detective Rob Hemmert took the initiative of enhancing the databases that are used by law enforcement to investigate crimes.

"What they have done in Florida is to focus their energy on improving the content and quality of the databases that investigate criminal profiles. A critical piece is working with the I.T. division. That has been phenomenal because of what they did in Central Florida, and that now exists in every county in Central Florida. When a crime is committed, regardless of age, they enter the specifics, kind of crime, instruments and tools, and whether they knew the suspects. So if even if a juvenile criminal who committed a violent crime was eight or nine or ten years old, it remains available to law enforcement. This is now a matter of practice in Florida."

What that means is that, in Central Florida, for example, if an investigator is in Brevard County, he or she can pull up, on his or her laptop, information that is of a similar nature, and can see if anyone living in that community has that kind of alignment.

Peggy Moore, Michelle's good friend, wrote an addendum to the initiative to include the law and its applications.

Peggy has an ample background from which to draw her knowledge. She was a two-term mayorally appointed commissioner for the City of

Annapolis Housing Authority. She also served on the board for Psycho-therapeutic Treatment Services from 1991 to 1999 in Annapolis. This was a private organization that provided transitional housing for mentally challenged individuals. Peggy then went to work for American Communities Property Trust, a publicly traded real-estate holdings, land development, and property management company. She was vice president of US Operations until the company was sold in 2010, and then she moved back to Florida, but stayed on with the operation as a consultant for two years.

She titled her addendum: *Michelle Lynn's Law Initiative.* It reads as follows:

"Charlie Brandt killed his pregnant mother at age thirteen. He was institutionalized for a year and released back into his father's custody. Psychiatric reports indicated he should have been monitored; however, there was nothing left of Charlie Brandt to follow. It was as if the slate were wiped clean. Even his younger sisters were unaware he'd killed their mother. They believed their mother died in a car accident. It wasn't until his family was contacted about the murders and Charlie's suicide that they became aware he murdered their mother.

The *Michelle Lynn Jones Foundation* has been set up to increase public awareness about invisible criminals. An awareness that someone, living next door to you, and unbeknownst to you, might be a criminal responsible for violent crimes. We all deserve the right to protect ourselves from the enemy—from becoming victims ourselves. However, in the case of Charlie Brandt, he was a minor, so his file was sealed. Any government agency doing a background check on Charlie would have discovered nothing of a criminal nature. Now, the tragic events of 911 created new policies, and opened some doors for deeper investigations. However, the law still states that a minor has full rights of file confidentiality, regardless of the type of crime they committed.

The *Michelle Lynn Jones Initiative* acknowledges that we need to protect our young people in society from becoming stigmatized, or stifling their future due to a mistake they made during a time when they were under eighteen, such as shoplifting. Shoplifting results from a poor decision made by a minor, but not one causing bodily harm to others. We believe if a minor commits a violent crime, specifically murder or rape, they do not have the right of non-disclosure and confidentiality. We believe that at the very minimum, law enforcement agencies should have access to that information.

There are many law enforcement agencies that have begun to network and have created global-protected sites that allow them to have access to view or upload information about crimes committed by anyone of any age, information vital to keeping people safe.

The catch is that this is not the law. Everything law enforcement is doing is on their own terms, creating their own initiative, and flying under the radar in order to better protect society. The issue with the efforts of some law enforcement agencies is that they are not comprehensive and it is not backed by a law requiring agencies to undertake them. Not all law enforcement agencies participate. and anything committed prior to the initial date the agency commenced their initiative is not included. They should have access to any information that would be considered vital to the safety and well-being of the public.

It is important to know that if Charlie Brandt's juvenile record was not sealed, his victims would probably be alive today, most certainly Michelle Jones. When Charlie Brandt killed a woman under a bridge a few blocks from his home, a witness saw him running across the street and this witness assisted law enforcement in creating a sketch of the person the witness saw. The sketch had an uncanny resemblance to Charlie Brandt. If law enforcement were able to look at Charlie's record, they would have investigated him.

We need to protect the rights of our children. We also need to protect the rights of every citizen. In order to do this, there has to be a compromise. A compromise that is based on common sense. Statistics have proven that violent criminals go on to repeat their crimes 65 percent of the time. The initiative for *Michelle Lynn's Law* has been created to draw public awareness and support to have the current laws examined and re-orchestrated to better protect society. We have modern technology that enables us to better gather facts and support the reasons why a change is not only needed but forthcoming. We need your support. To be a voice in our initiative to create change, friend Friends of Michelle Lynn Jones on Facebook; by doing so, you will be signing a petition to support change in our current legal system that will allow law enforcement agencies the ability to have access to all violent criminals in their databases. Maybe you have a Charlie Brandt living in your neighborhood. Shouldn't you have the right to know?"

Christine Dumouchel became friends with Michelle Jones in junior high school. "Michelle and I were really close friends growing up," Christine said. "I lived close to their house and Bill and Mary Lou were like my parents." Christine remembered meeting Charlie, and the impression he left on her was not good. "I met him once when I was young. And I remember thinking, 'He is creepy.' Michelle told me, 'That's my uncle, he's all right.' And I thought she might be embarrassed, but I sensed that something was not right with him." Uncle Charlie suddenly sounded like the unsavory, lurking villain in Alfred Hitchcock's "*Shadow of a Doubt.*"

Then Michelle left for college early, and the two girls lost touch. "Then, when I went on Facebook years later and I looked her up. I found out she had passed away, and I started to cry. And then I looked up Deb Knight, and Deb told me to talk to the Joneses, Bill and Mary Lou. They gave me the DVD with the "*48 Hour*" and it destroyed me. I did not go to work for four days," stated the childhood friend, her voice cracking a bit. "Now I am very committed to the initiative, because it needs to be out there, and I am doing everything in my power to help get it out there."

Mary Lou Jones mentioned the area of legislation as being the third area covered by the original initiative. "It's legislation to provide these databases to the public, but that is the area that doesn't take that much precedence now, because it is actually happening because of all the global information." Michelle's mother was referring to all the social media, as well as search engines and background searches, available for free.

But would Mary Lou have run a background check on Charlie when she found out he was marrying her sister Teri?

"I don't know that I would have done a background check on Charlie in 1986, but today, knowing what I know, I would definitely do it. I have talked to people who have done this with others who have come into their families. Look at what happened in Newtown, Connecticut, and in some other places."

The mother and nurse, who is still practicing, thinks there are a number of factors that contribute to violence in our world today. "And the horrific things that are occurring go beyond the evil that some do, not to minimize what Charlie did. As President Obama said when Newtown occurred, there are multiple forces in place that need attention. It is going to take a multifaceted approach. I subscribe to the President's statement."

There is still an unknown, even more terrifying factor, and Mary Lou is not afraid to name it.

"How do you discover that *before* they have committed a crime? How do you know? How do you discover that about a person? I don't know that you can. That said, how do you protect people? That's where I have trouble. How do I protect someone from a Charlie? How could I have protected Michelle and Teri from Charlie?"

In 2005, one year after Michelle's death, her mother, her father, and her brother wrote her the following letter. It was published in *The Orlando Sentinel*.

Dearest Daughter and Sister—Michelle,

It is so hard to believe that a year has passed since you left this world! How shocked your Dad, Sean and I were then! We miss you terribly and each of our hearts has a hole that can never be filled. We do look forward to our reunion someday...oh what a joyful day that will be. We continue to feel so empty without your loving, vibrant life!!! You were so engaged, so centered on living life. Your Grandma Jones has been quite strong, turning ninety this year and often talks of the special love she has for you. Your kitties are growing! Gizzie Girl is bringing lots of love to Diana and her family. And Kole has become a special joy to us with his loving nature and joined Kodi and Chloe at home. Your aunts and uncles have all shared this loss as well. Along with them, your cousins and their families have been deeply saddened by your passing.

You introduced us to friends that we will remain in touch with throughout the rest of our lives, as you would have. There are so many of them…but we have been in contact with the Musketeers and their families often to provide support, share our painful journey, and begin to regain hope for the future:

Debbie, Pat, Tye, Brooke, and Chloe; Tammy, Terry, Starr, and Haven; Peg, Joe, Tanner, Luke, Ingrid, and Maddie; Diana and JD, Taylor, Ryan, and Connor; Lisa Emmons, Hanna and Troop; Dawn, Donnie, and Darbie; and Jimmy Finch has also been supportive. We've been especially blessed by the continued support from Chester and Carol Wheeler and their families. Sue Heard, from TGC family, has called often, to express ongoing support from this organization. And your special colleagues/friends developed in TGC work, Suzy and Cam, and Nicole and Mark, along with their staff, have contacted us often to offer support and encouragement.

While our hearts are so sad and many tears have been shed because of the pain of losing you, we are making every effort to add meaning to your life. Yes, for as long as we live, we will focus our time and energy to make a difference in the lives of individuals and families. . .to make the world a safer place.

You would want us to focus on these efforts as you valued the principles of trust so deeply and shared this conviction with us on many occasions.

We will not say goodbye to you, our special angel...as we believe you are with us in spirit always.

Sending our Love over spiritual pathways to You,

Mom, Dad, and Sean

Kodi, Kole, and Chloe

...and your Gizzie Girl

In Loving Memory of
Michelle Lynn Jones,
September 17, 1966—September 13, 2004

For her part, Mary Lou remembers, and probably will always remember, the card that Michelle, the daughter she would have wanted desperately to protect, made for her.

Mary Lou writes:

"This was a card , made of purple construction paper, that Michelle gave me when she was 12 (1978)...."

Someone's important and that is plain to see.
Someone's smile is magic and lights the world for me.
Someone always cheers me and things seem bright and new.
Can you guess that "someone"?
Mother it's you!
Mother, I am happy where you are happy too.
I know you will help me to grow up strong and true.
Mother, I am trying to do and say and be
All the things that make you feel proud of me.

Michelle Jones was writing her autobiography for a school project when she was twelve years old.

She titled it, "One Life to Live."

The timing of death, like the ending of a story, gives a changed meaning to what preceded it. — Mary Catherine Bateson

One

Life

to

Live

by: Michelle
Jones

Publisher: Chelle Jo Company

Place of Publication:
Longwood, Florida

Copyright Date: 1978

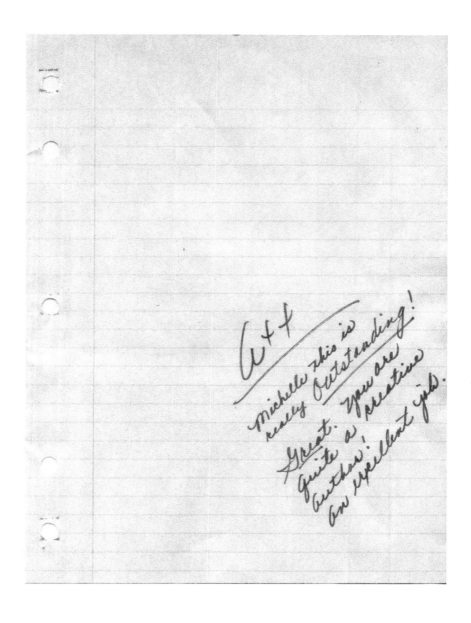

Dedication

I dedicate the story of my life to my dear parents.

Table of Contents

<u>Table of Illustrations</u>   pgs

①.

Before I was born
1965-1966

Bill and Mary Lou
Jones, my parents were
married at St. John's
Catholic Church in Clinton,
Maryland. They were
married on June 6, 1965 on
a beautiful sunny (95°)
Sunday afternoon. For
their honeymoon they
went to Dallas, Pennsylvania.

My father was in the
Air Intelligence Division of
the Navy stationed on the
U.S.S. Franklin Delano
Roosevelt, an aircraft carrier.
On June 16, 1965 my father
went back to the ship and
sailed to the Mediterranean
for a six month cruise. He
visited such countries as
Spain, France, Italy,
Turkey and the Islands of
Mallorca, Capri and Crete.

My mother had
completed nursing school
and was working in the
Coronary Care and Medical
Intensive Care Unit at
the Washington Hospital
Center in Washington D.C.
during the time my
father was in the Navy.

My parents went on a
couple short trips the year
before I was born. In
February 1966 they went
to Williamsburg, Va. to
celebrate the fact that
they were going to be
parents. My mother had
an upset stomach a few
times while they were
away.

In June 1966 my
parents went to White
Lake, N.C., a resort to
celebrate their first
wedding anniversary.

③

They had made plans to go on a camping trip, but were in a car accident, June 14, 1966. Fortunately no one was hurt, but our car of 9 months was completely destroyed and had to be replaced.

My father again had to go on a 7 month cruise to the Pacific Ocean near Vietnam. With this trip and his subsequent trip home, he was able to travel around the world.

My mother transferred to the Maternity Unit at Washington Hospital Center in May 1966 to get some good experience in being a mother. She continued to work there unil August 28, 1966.

(4.)

First Year of My Life

My birthday was on a beautiful sunny Saturday afternoon September 17, 1966 at 5:36 P.M.. My statistics were 6 lbs. 10 oz., 19½" long. My grandmother and my grandfather informed the American Red Cross so that they could notify my father who was on the USS F.D. Roosevelt, an aircraft carrier in the Pacific Ocean enroute to Japan.

My father was so happy that I was healthy and a girl. He and some of his Navy co-workers went to Tokyo to celebrate my birth. They went to the Imperial Hotel for dinner and the band played "Michelle" for their first song of the evening.

My mother was both very happy and sad, too.

⑤

She was so proud to have such a healthy, beautiful baby girl. But she was sad too, because my father could not be with us. It wasn't until January 13, 1967 that my dad came home from the Navy. We were so excited.

Between the time of my arrival and my dad's return from the Navy mom and I stayed at Grandmother Helfrich's house in Clinton, Maryland.

Below, is me wearing my Japanese pajamas that my dad sent me from Tokyo, Japan.   over → First photo

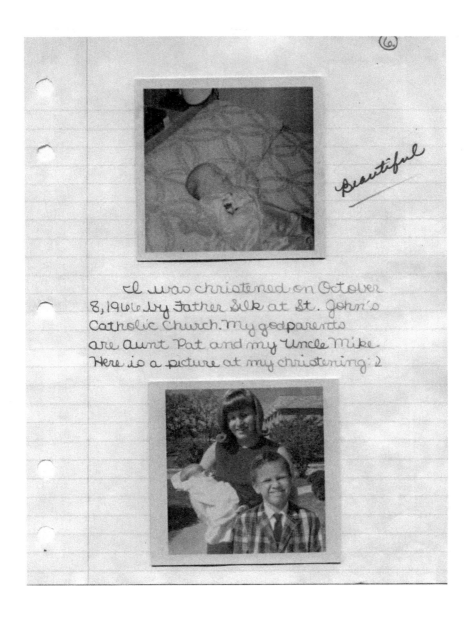

I was christened on October 8, 1966 by Father Silk at St. John's Catholic Church. My godparents are Aunt Pat and my Uncle Mike. Here is a picture at my christening: 2

⑦

My first Christmas was really exciting. All of my mom's sisters and brother were home plus my dad's brother and a family friend were house guests. I received lots of stuffed animals. In this picture below I have a few of my stuffed animals.

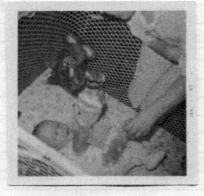

8.

My mom, dad and I then moved into our very first home in February of 1967.

My dad went to work for the Washington Gas Light Company as a draftsman. My mom went to work in a convalescent nursing care center.

It was so much fun being a family. I had my first bedroom and lots of toys. We visited both sets of grandparents often.

In June of 1967, my Aunt Pat (my mom's sister) and my Uncle Ray (my dad's brother) were married.

⑨

Second Year of My Life

On September 17, 1967, my first birthday, all of my immediate family and my close relatives came to our apartment for a buffet dinner and a birthday party. My mother made me a bunny cake, which was decorated with coconut and colored pink. My parents gave me a section of my bunny in which I stuck my face. In the picture below is me and the section of the bunny. I had not yet got to the point of sticking my face in the bunny.

⑩

My mom went to work in the Maternity Department at Cafritz Memorial Hospital.

On my second Christmas my mom and I were with my dad for the first time. On Christmas Day, I received a rocking chair, a matching toybox, a few dolls, and some nice new clothes. I was so excited to be with both my mother and father.

On February 22, 1968 (Washington's Birthday), I had two new cousins, which were twins. They are my double-first cousin's because their mom (my Aunt Pat) is my mom's sister and their father (my Uncle Ray) is my dad's brother. In the picture on the next page is one of them. Her name is Kim.

(11.)

My other cousin is Chris.
Kim is in the picture.

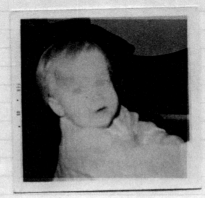

   On the summer of
1968 we went on our
first vacation, which
was 2 weeks long. On
vacation we went and visited
Aunt Pat, Uncle Ray and
my double-first cousins,
Chris and Kim, then we
went to Orlando and then
to Daytona Beach for 5
days.

12.

Third Year of My Life

On September 17, 1968, my second birthday, I became 2 years old. I had a wonderful birthday.

In October, 1968 after my Aunt Claudia was married, we took a trip up to visit my greatgrandmother and to see my Great Aunt Mary. In the picture below are me, my mother, my Aunt Claudia and my Great Aunt Mary.

(13.)

In May of 1969, my Aunt Claudia gave birth to a healthy baby boy. My aunt and her husband named him, Robbie.

One week in July, 1969, we went to a Family Reunion of the Brown's at my Aunt Judy's and my Uncle Bill's House. My mom's mother is a member of the Brown family.

⑭.

Fourth Year of My Life

On September 17, 1969, my third birthday, I became 3 years old. I got lots of gifts from friends and my relatives.

In November of 1969 we moved to Orlando, Florida, my address is: 2597 Telstar Avenue and my phone number is: 423-8475. My first house that my mom, my dad and me had lived in. We hadn't lived there long and I got a Beagle Terrier dog that I named Snooks. My very first and my own animal. In the picture on the next page is my puppy.

over → first photo

(15.)

Isn't she cute!

Later, I started
Nursery School at Snow
White Academy. I had
lots of fun.
My first Christmas
in Florida my Aunt Paula,
my Uncle Terry, my Aunt
Pat, my Uncle Ray and my
four (4) cousins: Debbie, Bill,
Chris and Kim. My Aunt
Pat, my Uncle Ray and
the twins stayed with
us because they had a

(16.)

fire in their house.
In the summer of
1970 my grandmother and
grandfather came to our
house on surprise and
brought their children,
Teri and Mike. We had
alot of fun while they
were here.

(17)

Fifth Year of My Life

On September 17, 1970, my fourth birthday, I became 4 years old. All that we did for my 4th birthday is eat ice cream and cake. I did not have a real big party.

In Christmas of 1970 we went to Maryland, to my grandmother's house. We had fun.

In April of 1971 my Aunt Claudia gave birth to her second child. It was a healthy baby boy. My aunt and her husband named him Tony, after my grandfather.

In July of 1971, we got our second dog. He was a black poodle with a silver face and silver paws. My family and I named him Jacque. He

(18.)

is a very playful dog. In
the picture below is
my dog, Jacque.

When we got Jacque my
Aunt Claudia, Uncle Mike
and my cousins were here.
While they were here we
went to Busch Gardens,
and we had alot of fun.

(19.)

Sixth Year of My Life

On September 17, 1971, my fifth birthday, I then became 5 years old.

I started Kindergarten at Snow White Academy. While I was in Kindergarten our whole class got our picture taken on a pony. In the photo below is me on the pony.

Love these western movie stars!

20.

In Christmas of 1971, my family and I went to Maryland to spend the holidays. There was alot of snow to play in, which I did most of the time. We had so much fun.

In the summer of 1972, we went to Rock Springs and New Smyrna Beach with our friends. In the picture below we are at Rock Springs with our friends.

(21)

Seventh Year of My Life

On September 17, 1972, my sixth birthday, I turned 6 years old. For my sixth birthday, I had a birthday party. I had 8 people over to celebrate. In the photo below are the people.

I started First Grade at Catalina Elementary School. Miss Hazlip was my teacher.

On September 29, 1972, my mom gave birth to a healthy baby boy. My parents named him Sean.

Later, my dad went into the hospital. He was in the hospital because of a Kidney Problem. We were very upset.

In Christmas of 1972, I was with my dad, my mom, my brother and my grandparents. We had a wonderful Christmas.

During the summer of 1973, my family and some good friends of ours went to Rock Springs every weekend. We also went to New Smyrna alot with them. We had alot of fun. In the picture on the next page is us at Rock Springs.   →

24

Eighth Year of My Life

On September 17, 1973, my seventh birthday, I turned 7 years old. I had some friends over for my birthday.

I then went to second grade at Catalina Elementary School. Mrs. Randolph was my teacher. While I was in school, I joined the Brownies. We went many places such as: Moss Park and Holiday Hospital.

On September 29, 1973, my brother's first birthday, we were out in our trailer at Outdoor Resorts. He also had a bunny cake except is was blue. He stuck his face in the cake, too. He had alot of fun.

25.

In Christmas of 1973, I was with my mother, my father, my brother and my grandparents were there. We had alot of fun that Christmas.

In May of 1974, I received my First Communion. That was scary!

In the summer of 1974, we went to Maryland with our new trailer. We also took our trailer to Fort Wilderness. In the photograph on the next page is my aunt Teri in Maryland at Solomon's Island.

(27)

Ninth Year of My Life

On September 17, 1974, my eighth birthday, I turned eight (8) years old. For my eighth birthday, my family and I went to Walt Disney World and we had so much fun.

When I was eight, I started third grade and changed from a public school, to a private. I went to St. John Vianney's and my teacher was Mrs. Aurand. She was very nice.

On September 29, 1974, my brother turned 2. For his second birthday we had some friends over for ice cream and cake. He became brattier by the minute.

28.

In October, I
started playing the
Organ. I took my
lessons at Winter
Park School of Music
(Keller Music) in the
Winter Park Mall.
My teacher was Mrs.
Blais.

In Christmas of
1974 we went to
Maryland for 2 weeks
over the holidays. We
had so much fun.

In January of 1975,
we bought another
dog. She is a girl and
we named her Cheri.
She is a black poodle.
In the picture on the
next page is my new
dog, Cheri. She is the one
on the right side.

In the summer of 1975, I went to Camp Ticochee with two other friends. We had alot of fun. While I was at camp, my parents wrote me a letter saying they had a surprise for me when I got home. When I got home it was a new station wagon. I was very happy.

(30)

Tenth Year of My Life

On September 17, 1975, my ninth birthday, I turned nine (9) years old. We had a few friends over for cake and ice cream. I had alot of fun with my friends.

On September 28, 1975 we moved to Brantly Harbor. I made many new friends. I also changed schools again. I went to Forest City for fourth grade. I made so many friends it was unbelievable. I liked fourth grade.

On September 29, 1975, my brother turned 3 years old. By this time he was brattier than ever.

In Christmas of 1975, I was with my mom, my

dad, my brother, and my
grandparents. I received
a 3-speed bike. In the
evening on Christmas, we
had a big turkey dinner.
    In summer of 1976,
we didn't go anywhere
special except for going
to attractions. We still
had fun.

Eleventh Year of My Life

On September 17, 1976, my tenth birthday. I turned 10 years old. Boy, is life going by quickly. My family and I had a few friends come over. That was a good birthday. I enjoyed it alot.

When I was ten I started fifth grade. My teacher, Mrs. Fry was very nice. I had so much fun that year. While I was in fifth grade my Aunt Teri lived with us. She went to Jones College. I like her because she is funny and very nice.

In Christmas of 1976, my mom's brother and sisters and her parents were here. I had 3 aunts,

(33)

1 uncle, 4 cousins, and my grandparents staying at our house. We had a very large Christmas that year. My cousins, my brother, and I had lots of fun. My aunts, my uncle, and my grandparents were here until January 2, 1977.

In May of 1977, I had a hamster that died. When I got another small animal, I got a guinea pig. My guinea pig is a boy, dark brown, and his name is Pierre. Then in June, I got another guinea pig. This time, I got a girl. She is orange white, and her name is Fe-Fe.

In the summer of 1977, my family and I went to Mississippi.

In July of 1977, my guinea pig, Fie-Fie died. She died of Sepsis and Septic arthritis. I was very unhappy. About a week after Fie-Fie's death, my mom and dad bought me another guinea pig. I was very happy that it was a girl. She is also orange and white. I named her Gi-Gi. In the photo below is my brother with them.

On August 19, 1977 my dog, Cheri had puppies. They were the cutest little things you have ever seen. There were 3 puppies, 2 girls and 1 boy. One of the girls was black, the other girl was brown, and the boy was black. In the photo below, there are the three puppies and the mommy.

Twelfth Year of My Life

On September 17, 1977, my eleventh birthday, I became 11 years old. For this year, I had a slumber party. It was fun!

Now, I am 11. I finished Forest City Elementary, so now I go to Teague Middle School and I am in the sixth grade. In the photo on the side is me on the first day of sixth grade. In a full school day you go through six periods, which are an hour

(37)

long each. Here is my
schedule:

1. Enrichment (Music) - Mrs.
   Gore
2. Social Studies - Mrs.
   Lambert
3. Mathematics - Mrs. Sticka
4. English - Mrs. O'Hara
5. Physical Education -
   Miss Moloney
6. Science - Mrs. Jake

I like my schedule
arranged this way. I
like school very much.

This past Christmas,
I was with my mom,
my dad, and my
brother. We had a
nice Christmas. On
December 26, 1977, my
mom's parents arrived at
our house. My family

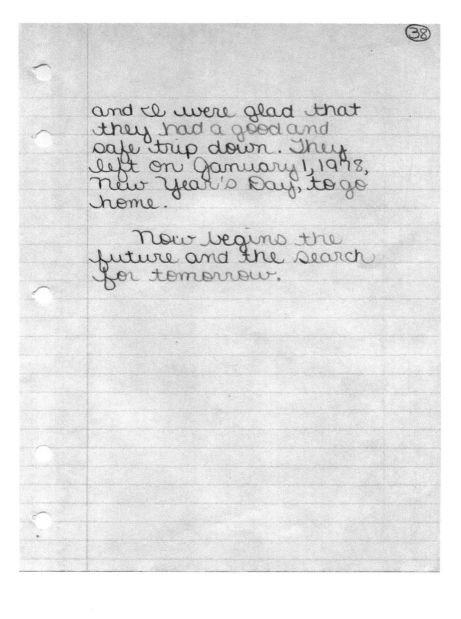

38

and I were glad that
they had a good and
safe trip down. They
left on January 1, 1978,
New Year's Day, to go
home.

Now begins the
future and the search
for tomorrow.

(Herald Photo by Elda Nichols)

PLANTING
POINTERS

2/23/77

Some of that Florida weather seems to have reappeared and all that's needed now is rain for Michelle Jones and other would-be planters. Michelle and Kelli Leete, a fellow fifth-grader at Forest City Elementary School, won second place in the Florida Arbor Day poster contest. The prize: $75 worth of shrubs which, weather permitting, the school's PTO will be planting, courtesy of Bolling Farms of Longwood. The contest was sponsored by the Orlando Area Chamber of Commerce.

ABOUT THE AUTHORS

Diana Montane is a journalist and best-selling author. She began her career at Miami's first newspaper, The Miami News, and continued as Entertainment Editor of EXITO, a Spanish language weekly published by The Chicago Tribune.

Diana co-authored the autobiography of talk show host Cristina, My Life as a Blonde, published by Warner Books. She also co-authored the best-selling and impacting The Daughters of Juarez, with Univision anchor Teresa Rodriguez, published by Simon & Schuster. I Would Find a Girl Walking published by Penguin, with crime journalist Kathy Kelly was also a bestseller. Missing and Presumed Dead, about psychic Gale St. John and her searches for missing persons with her cadaver dogs, will be published by Llewellyn and released in 2014.

Invisible Killer is Sean Robbins' inaugural entry into the world of true crime writers. A new talent, Robbins is a former recording artist with The Autumn Offering. With an insatiable drive to create, he has written numerous short stories, poems, and screenplays. Invisible Killer is his first book co-authorship, launching his unflinching style. He resides in Daytona Beach, Florida, where he writes full-time.